'In current ecumenical dialogue, th[...]
with disputed points either left to one[...]
Dr De Chirico takes issue with this approach and argues that the questions that divided the Western Church in the sixteenth century have not gone away and must still be faced. Evangelicals and Catholics hold some things in common but, as this book shows, their differences are important and cannot be overlooked.'
Gerald Bray, Research Professor of Divinity, Beeson Divinity School, Alabama, USA, and Director of Research, Latimer Trust

'In this helpful book, my friend Leonardo De Chirico proves why he is one of the pre-eminent Protestant scholars of Roman Catholicism. He accomplishes just what he sets out to prove: that even though Protestants and Catholics may use similar words, they believe in very different gospels. As he accomplishes this, he displays his characteristic wisdom, charity, kindness and expansive knowledge of both Protestant and Catholic doctrine.'
Tim Challies, <www.challies.com>

'This is a challenging read which sets out the crucial doctrinal differences between Roman Catholicism and Protestantism, especially those hiding within some apparent verbal similarities. It is a provocative counterpoint to the sometimes naive ecumenical thrust of much modern discussion on inter-church relations.'
Dr Lee Gatiss, Director, Church Society, and author of *Light after Darkness: How the reformers regained, retold, and relied on the gospel of grace*

'How can I stand next to my Roman Catholic friend and say the words, "We believe in the one, holy, catholic and apostolic faith" and mean something completely different by the words: "we", "believe", "in", "the one", "holy", "catholic", "apostolic" and "faith"?

De Chirico, an Italian national and church planter in Rome, is better placed than anyone to act as a bridge between evangelicals and Roman Catholics. This book provides the key to understanding these differences, avoiding pitfalls and communicating more effectively with Roman Catholics.

De Chirico's book is a powerful tool to help us talk about the Jesus whom we love with the people in our lives whom we love who live in a world influenced by Roman Catholicism.'
The Revd Dr Mark Gilbert, Catholic evangelist, Sydney, Australia

'I am thrilled to see this new book by Leonardo De Chirico. I benefited immensely from reading De Chirico's doctoral thesis several years ago on Roman Catholicism. As one who teaches theology, including a course on the church fathers and medieval theology, it is tempting to say that Rome and Protestantism simply agree on many things. But I have been persuaded by De Chirico's analysis that central tenets of Roman Catholicism put even seemingly common theological territory in a different light. If you want to understand the deep principles of Roman Catholic theology, I strongly encourage the reading of this book.'
Bradley G. Green, Professor of Theological Studies, Union University, Jackson, Tennessee, USA

'This book is easily the most profound analysis of the Roman Catholic "world" available today. The fact that it is also the most lucid and accessible makes it remarkable. In a measured and eirenic way, the author peels back the subtle deceptions through which, over the best part of two millennia, the Papacy has misrepresented the Christian faith.'
Ranald Macaulay, founder, Christian Heritage

'Leonardo De Chirico's *Same Words, Different Worlds* is an authoritative, clear and compelling account. He knows of what he speaks: fluffy minded evangelicals confused about "contemporary" Roman Catholicism, read and learn.'
Dr Josh Moody (PhD, University of Cambridge), Senior Pastor, College Church, and President, God Centered Life Ministries

'Labouring for the gospel in the shadow of the Vatican, Dr De Chirico knows Roman Catholicism of the past and present, its doctrine and practice, its US and global identity. He then adds his deep knowledge of the historical orthodox Christian faith. And he then adds his winsome and gracious nature. The result is a book that with clarity and grace shows the profound difference between Roman Catholicism and evangelicalism – and why that difference is of such ultimate, eternal significance.'

Stephen J. Nichols, President, Reformation Bible College, Chief Academic Officer, Ligonier Ministries, and author of *R. C. Sproul: A life*

'When Vatican II met at Rome between 1962 and1965, global Protestants were helped to assess the developments taking place there through "observers", invited from various communions. In more recent times, this service has been admirably fulfilled by Leonardo De Chirico who, by his on-site residence and his digesting of fresh papal pronouncements and activity today serves as the eyes and ears of evangelical Protestants globally. Now, in *Same Words, Different Worlds*, De Chirico offers us a fine distillation of his observations.'

Kenneth J. Stewart, Emeritus Professor of Theological Studies, Covenant College, Georgia, USA

SAME WORDS, DIFFERENT WORLDS

Leonardo De Chirico (PhD, King's College London) is the pastor of Breccia di Roma, lecturer in Historical Theology at the Istituto di Formazione Evangelica e Documentazione (IFED) in Padua, Italy, and the director of the Reformanda Initiative. Additionally, he blogs at <www.vaticanfiles.org>. He is the director of *Studi di Teologia*, an evangelical theological journal that has been in publication in Italy for forty years, and the author of *Evangelical Theological Perspectives on Post-Vatican II Roman Catholicism* (2003), *A Christian's Pocket Guide to the Papacy: Its origin and role in the 21st century* (2015) and *A Christian's Pocket Guide to Mary: Mother of God?* (2017).

SAME WORDS, DIFFERENT WORLDS

Do Roman Catholics and evangelicals
believe the same gospel?

Leonardo De Chirico

INTER-VARSITY PRESS
36 Causton Street, London SW1P 4ST, England
Email: ivp@ivpbooks.com
Website: www.ivpbooks.com

First published 2021

British Library Cataloguing-in-Publication Data
A catalogue record for this book is available from the British Library.

ISBN: 978-1-78974-360-9
eBook ISBN: 978-1-78974-361-6

Set in 11/14pt Minion Pro
Typeset in Great Britain by CRB Associates, Potterhanworth, Lincolnshire
Printed in Great Britain by Ashford Colour Ltd, Gosport, Hampshire

Produced on paper from sustainable sources

*Inter-Varsity Press publishes Christian books that are true to the Bible and that communicate
the gospel, develop discipleship and strengthen the church for its mission in the world.*

*IVP originated within the Inter-Varsity Fellowship, now the Universities and Colleges Christian
Fellowship, a student movement connecting Christian Unions in universities and colleges
throughout Great Britain, and a member movement of the International Fellowship
of Evangelical Students. Website: www.uccf.org.uk. That historic association is maintained,
and all senior IVP staff and committee members subscribe to the UCCF Basis of Faith.*

Contents

Foreword

Fussy. Divisive. Quarrelsome. Those are the sort of words that come to mind when anyone flags up differences of belief these days. Most of us have grown so acclimatized to our post-truth culture that our minds have dulled to differentiation. And a simple appeal to 'grace' or 'tolerance' is usually enough to snap us out of any brief moments of discernment.

So, when it comes to the differences between Protestants and Roman Catholics, most Christians instinctively warm to Samuel Johnson when he said, 'For my part, Sir, I think all Christians, whether Papists or Protestants, agree in the essential articles, and that their differences are trivial, and rather political than religious.' The distinction between justification by faith (Rome's position) and justification by faith *alone* (the Protestant view) is heard as the sort of pernickety squabble that could only interest pedants with a taste for prickliness.

With the courteous graciousness and keen insight he is known for, Leonardo De Chirico shows us here just how much we are missing. Laying out the underlying theological framework of Roman Catholicism, he shows how Rome can use words familiar to evangelicals ('grace', 'faith', 'justification' etc.), but intend quite different things by them. What becomes very clear is that Rome does not just add a few of its own sprinkles (Mary, purgatory and the pope) to an otherwise broadly agreed gospel. From bottom to top, it is a cake with a different (if similar-sounding) recipe and different (if similar-sounding) ingredients. With this book, then, Dr De Chirico switches on the lights to help us think rightly about Roman Catholicism and engage Roman Catholic friends with biblical grace and biblical clarity.

But this book actually does something more, something that makes it valuable for all evangelicals, whether or not they ever talk with Roman Catholics. It is this: just as Luther's own debates with Rome clarified his theology, so this book helps evangelicals to think more clearly about the gospel and so helps us be more truly evangelical.

Take, for example, Dr De Chirico's astute explanation of the vital word *hapax* ('once for all'). *Hapax* or *ephapax* is a word used frequently in the New Testament of the work of Christ, especially in Hebrews as it contrasts the repeated (and so insufficient) sacrifices of the law with the single (and so sufficient) sacrifice of Christ. It is a word that takes us to the heart of what makes the good news good. Because Christ's redemptive work is *hapax* and so entirely sufficient, the gospel is God's kind work of rescue, not his offer of assistance. It is not a call for the strong and good to prove themselves, but for the weak and bad to prove the depths of the mercy of Christ. Redemption is accomplished by Christ alone, and needs no topping up from us. The pastoral implications for guilty, weary Christians are huge, for it is only when we have grasped the finality of what God has said and done in Christ that we can rest on Christ alone and not ourselves. Only then can we boast only in the cross. Only then can we know true liberation.

In other words, this book not only gives us wisdom: it takes us deep into the joy-giving world of the gospel. If you would go further up and further in, take and read.

Michael Reeves
President and Professor of Theology
Union School of Theology

Acknowledgments

I wish to thank my brother in Christ, friend and colleague Clay Kannard for reading the manuscript before publication. He not only provided corrections to the English text but also offered insights into how to improve the book.

I also wish to dedicate this work to my fellow elders in the Chiese Evangeliche Riformate Battiste in Italia (<www.cerbi.it>), the Evangelical Reformed Baptist Churches in Italy, the association of churches in which I too have the privilege of ministering. I admire the evangelical commitment of my co-workers in the ministry and the way they model attachment to the Word of God, love for the church and concern for the gospel cause. In a country that is somewhat used to the 'same words' of the gospel (given the still very influential Roman Catholic background) but has produced a religious culture that is a 'different world' from the gospel, the challenge to be faithful to the biblical message and to remain hopeful is massive. Yesterday, today and tomorrow the assurance is that the gospel 'is the power of God for salvation to everyone who believes' (Rom. 1:16).

Abbreviations

AG   *Ad Gentes* (decree on the missionary activity of the church, Second Vatican Council, 1965)

CCC   *Catechism of the Catholic Church* (comprehensive exposition of Roman Catholic doctrine, 1992)

Denz.   Heinrich Denzinger and Adolf Schönmetzer (eds.), *Enchiridion symbolorum definitionum et declarationum de rebus fidei et morum* (Freiburg, Basel, Rome and Vienna: Herder, 1997) (standard Roman Catholic collection of magisterial texts)

DV   *Dei Verbum* (dogmatic constitution on divine revelation, Second Vatican Council, 1965)

ECT   *Evangelicals and Catholics Together* (US joint statement, 1994)

ECT   Evangelicals and Catholics Together (informal dialogue and initiative based in North America)

EG   *Evangelii Gaudium* (apostolic exhortation by Pope Francis, 2013)

GS   *Gaudium et Spes* (pastoral constitution on the church in the modern world, Second Vatican Council, 1965)

JDDJ   *Joint Declaration on the Doctrine of Justification* (Lutheran–Roman Catholic joint statement, 1999)

LG   *Lumen Gentium* (dogmatic constitution on the church, Second Vatican Council, 1964)

UR   *Unitatis Redintegratio* (decree on ecumenism, Second Vatican Council, 1964)

VD   *Verbum Domini* (apostolic exhortation by Pope Benedict XVI, 2010)

Introduction

It is often pointed out that evangelical Protestants and Roman Catholics have a lot in common. On the one hand, there is an apparent 'common orthodoxy' rooted in the ancient trinitarian and Christological creeds, which use the same basic words of the gospel: 'God', 'Jesus Christ', 'the Holy Spirit', 'the Bible', 'sin', 'faith', 'salvation', 'church' and so on. The shared vocabulary is for some an indication that there is much commonality. On the other hand, nobody can deny the profound differences that separate evangelical Protestants and Roman Catholics in their accounts of the doctrines of Christ, the church and salvation (i.e. the core of the gospel), as well as Mary, the intercession of the saints, purgatory, papal infallibility and the manifold practices that stem out of these. In many respects Roman Catholicism is really alien to the evangelical faith.

So, these faiths look somewhat similar, yet they are radically different. The question is: how can we meaningfully speak of the 'same' gospel if the two have core commitments that do not match? The problem lies with the way in which the same words are understood differently. They are the same phonetically – their pronunciations being equal – but in terms of theology they differ drastically. They have the same sounds, but they carry different meanings. The decisive issue is the frame of reference that binds them together.

As the Swiss linguist Ferdinand de Saussure (1857–1913) suggested concerning general linguistics, a distinction needs to be made between *langue* (language) and *parole* (word). Language is a signifying system that gives meaning to words. The latter are not free-floating items but receive their meaning in the context of the system in which they are used. In loose analogy, Roman Catholicism and the evangelical Protestant faith are two theological *langues* (languages) using similar *paroles* (words). If we apply our analysis to the concrete, individual words without grasping the theological framework in which they are located, we will miss the point. The resulting picture will be misleading and ultimately wrong.

This book will try to show why the Roman Catholic words are similar to those of the gospel and yet the Roman Catholic language is different from the gospel's language. The underlying theological framework of Roman Catholicism is not committed to the biblical gospel and therefore the words it uses are twisted and understood differently. The truth claims of Rome and the justification of its practices are presented in seemingly biblical language, yet they can hardly be considered as biblical on closer analysis. How is this possible? And how can this explosive claim be substantiated?

The first chapter will sketch several common viewpoints that are increasingly adopted in the ecumenical understanding of what is at stake between evangelicals and Catholics today. Much of what is wrongly assumed has to do with an ever-present confusion: giving credit to the similarity of vocabulary taken out of biblical, theological and historical context. The chapter will suggest better interpretations of present-day trends in Roman Catholic ecumenism – a movement that seems to be so attractive to many evangelicals around the world. These interpretations are better because they fit the Roman Catholic system and therefore shed light on the way words are used.

The second and third chapters examine some key terms that are used in the Roman Catholic faith and are also common to evangelical language. The goal is to provide an introduction to their meaning in the context of the Roman Catholic system and to show how they differ from a faithful evangelical reading of Scripture and thus form a distinctively Roman Catholic world.

The fourth chapter will consider the two axes that form the backbone of the Roman Catholic system. It is around the nature–grace interdependence and the Christ–church interconnection that one can find the theological frame of reference that shapes Roman Catholic words. Roman Catholicism is pervaded by an attitude that is confident in the capacity of nature and matter to objectify grace (the bread that becomes Christ's body, the wine that becomes Christ's blood, the water of baptism and the oil of anointing that convey grace), in the ability of reason to develop a 'natural theology', in a person's ability to cooperate with and contribute to salvation through his or her own works, in the capacity of religions to be ways to God, in the capacity of the conscience to be the point of reference for truth, in the capacity of the pope to speak infallibly when he does so *ex cathedra* (with the full authority of office; literally 'from the chair'). In theological terms, according to this view, grace intervenes to 'elevate' nature to its supernatural end, relying on it and pre-supposing its untainted capacity to be elevated. Even if weakened by sin, nature maintains its ability to interface with grace because grace is indelibly inscribed in nature. Roman Catholicism does not distinguish between 'common grace' (with which God protects the world from sin) and 'special grace' (with which God saves the world) and, therefore, is pervaded by an optimistic belief that whatever is natural can be graced.

The Christ–church interconnection relies on the basic idea that, after the ascension of the risen Jesus Christ to the right hand of the Father, there is a sense in which Christ is 'really' present in his 'mystical body' (the church) which is inseparably connected to the hierarchical and papal institution of the Roman Church. For Roman Catholicism, the incarnation of Christ did not end with the ascension but is prolonged in the sacramental, institutional and teaching life of the church. The Roman Church exercises the royal, priestly and prophetic offices of Christ in the real and vicarious sense: through the priests who act *in persona Christi* (in the person of Christ), the church governs the world, dispenses grace and teaches the truth. The prerogatives of Christ are transposed into the self-understanding of the church: the power of the church is universal, the sacraments of the church transmit grace *ex opere operato* (by reason of them being enacted), the magisterium of the church is always true. The biblical distinction between 'head' (Christ) and 'members' (church) is confused in the category of *totus Christus* (the total Christ which includes both). The consequences of this confusion affect (and pollute) everything. The mystical–sacramental–institutional–papal church is conceived in an inflated, abnormal way.

Roman Catholicism lies within these two axes; the underlying optimism based on the interdependence between nature and grace corresponds to the leading role of the Roman ecclesiastical institution based on the interconnection between Christ and the church. The ultimate problem of Roman Catholicism is that it is not committed to the biblical gospel but to a spurious synthesis of Yes and No responses to it. This Yes and No pattern is embedded in all its expressions.

As the great Welsh preacher Martyn Lloyd-Jones (1899–1981) said, in Roman Catholicism 'it is not so much a denial of the truth that comes to pass as the addition to the truth which becomes a departure from it'.[1] If you affirm something of the gospel and add something else to it, you depart from the Christian faith altogether. Given this matrix that lies at the core of what Roman Catholicism stands for, every word used by Rome, even if it comes from the Bible, is marred by what is added to it and by the way it is connected with other biblically defective words. The result is a framework of reference that can hardly resemble the biblical faith that is taught in Scripture.

In dealing with Roman Catholicism, especially in times of mounting ecumenical pressure to acknowledge that we have the 'same' gospel and therefore we can be committed to the 'same' mission, evangelical Protestants should attempt to go beyond superficial commonalities based on the alleged shared vocabulary. They should instead be aware of the internal theological framework of Roman Catholic theology and try to understand it from within and in the light of Scripture. Roman Catholic theology is a complex yet coherent system that gives meaning to the words that are used. They sound like biblical terms but are inflated and distorted by external elements that make them substantially different from clear biblical teaching.

This book is being published eleven years after I launched the website <www.vaticanfiles.org>. It was in 2010 that I began writing the Vatican Files to assess and analyse Roman Catholic documents and

---

1 D. M. Lloyd-Jones, *Roman Catholicism* (London: Evangelical Press, n.d.), p. 3.

trends from an evangelical perspective. Since then more than 190 articles have been freely posted, offering an evangelical window into Roman Catholic theology and practice. In a sense, this book is a child of the Vatican Files since much of the material presented here originated there in one way or another. I still believe in the unique contribution of the Vatican Files to developing a robust evangelical discernment when dealing with Rome today.

1

Same words, same world? Questioning some common viewpoints

In our time, marked as it is by ecumenical friendliness and a general dislike for theological precision, there are a number of common views regarding Roman Catholicism and the evangelical Protestant faith that are quite widespread, both within and outside of the church. The prevailing impression is that the differences of the past are no longer as relevant as they have been for centuries. They are less stark and more nuanced than in times past. They are not black and white issues; they can be thought of as representing different shades of grey.

After all, do not evangelicals and Catholics share the bulk of the Christian faith, the Scriptures of the Old and the New Testaments (although with the difference of the deuterocanonical books), and the essential core of the gospel (superficially understood), while having remaining differences that do not preclude significant degrees of reconciliation and fellowship? There are people who actually argue that while evangelicals and Catholics have been divided in the past, they nonetheless share the 'same future'.[1]

These assumptions seem to be growing in plausibility and are gaining support from a variety of church circles. It is important to notice that they are built around a cluster of common ecumenical ideas that support one another, resulting in a convincing cumulative argument. In this chapter an attempt will be made to single them out (at least the most common ones) and to begin questioning them

1 T. P. Rausch (ed.), *Catholics and Evangelicals: Do they share a common future?* (New York, NY: Paulist Press, 2000).

one by one biblically, historically and theologically. Although arguing from different angles and highlighting various elements, we will see that the thread that weaves all these common viewpoints together is the use of the same words of the Christian faith. The impression is that the shared vocabulary is a strong pointer for the closeness of the Roman Catholic account of the gospel to the evangelical Protestant account.

Common viewpoint 1:
Evangelicals can embrace most
of the Roman Catholic *Catechism*

Understanding Roman Catholicism is high on the agenda of contemporary evangelical theologians. A lot of things are happening in the relationship between evangelicals and Catholics worldwide, leaving many observers perplexed and feeling the need to reflect theologically on the changing scenario. The widely acclaimed book *Is the Reformation Over? An evangelical assessment of Roman Catholicism* by Mark Noll and Carolyn Nystrom[2] focuses on this issue mainly in a North American context and traces the stunning developments that have taken place in recent decades, from the widespread anti-Catholic attitude of many evangelicals until the 1960s, to the growing convergence reflected in many bilateral dialogues between the Roman Church and different Protestant bodies from the late 1960s onwards. The North American 'Evangelicals and Catholics Together' (ECT) initiative is but one instance of such a historical turn.[3] In the light of the current situation, the authors ask themselves whether the Reformation is over and whether a new season of ecumenical rapprochement can be envisaged.

---

2 M. Noll and C. Nystrom, *Is the Reformation Over? An evangelical assessment of Roman Catholicism* (Grand Rapids, MI: Eerdmans, 2005).
3 A collection of all the ECT documents can be found in T. George and T. G. Guarino (eds.), *Evangelicals and Catholics Together at Twenty: Vital statements on contested topics* (Grand Rapids, MI: Brazos Press, 2015). For a critical assessement of ECT, see my article 'Christian unity vis-à-vis Roman Catholicism: a critique of the Evangelicals and Catholics Together dialogue', *Evangelical Review of Theology* 27.4 (2003), pp. 337–352.

In order to do that, Noll and Nystrom highlight the contents of the 1992 *Catechism of the Catholic Church*. Surveying the exposition of what Rome believes in this codified form, the authors argue that 'evangelicals can embrace at least two-thirds' of it.[4] This alleged consensus stems from 'common orthodoxy' based on the ancient trinitarian and Christological creeds: the triune nature of God, the incarnation of Jesus Christ as the God-man, the need for salvation, the reality of the church, the hope of eternal salvation and so on. The basic words of the gospel are the 'same' as those in the *Catechism*; for example, 'God', 'Jesus Christ', 'Bible', 'sin', 'faith', 'salvation'.

However, there is another side of the coin. As honest scholars, Noll and Nystrom later admit that when the *Catechism* speaks of Christ, it interweaves him with the church to the point of making them one,[5] which is unacceptable for evangelicals who consider the exaltation of a created reality an instance of idolatry. On this extension of the meaning of 'Christ' in the *Catechism* (i.e. the prolongation of his incarnation in the church), Rome builds its self-understanding of being a church endowed with the authority of Christ the King, the priesthood of Christ the Mediator and the truth of Christ the Prophet. But this is not what the gospel teaches. This is an inflated view of the church based on a defective view of Christ. On the one hand, then, there is an apparent 'common orthodoxy' based on the 'same' vocabulary of the seemingly shared trinitarian theology; on the other, there is a profound difference on the doctrine of Christ (and therefore the Trinity) which is the ground for the Church of Rome to claim the prerogatives of Christ in administering grace (through the sacraments), in exercising authority (through the hierarchical institution) and in teaching the truth (through the official teaching of popes, councils, etc.). The *Catechism* gives voice to *this* account of the Christian faith.[6]

---

4 Noll and Nystrom, *Is the Reformation Over?* p. 119.
5 Noll and Nystrom, *Is the Reformation Over?* pp. 147, 149.
6 For an evangelical assessement of the *Catechism*, see H. Carson, *The Faith of the Vatican: A fresh look at Roman Catholicism* (Darlington: Evangelical Press, 1996), and the more recent and thorough work by G. R. Allison, *Roman Catholic Theology and Practice: An evangelical assessment* (Wheaton, IL: Crossway, 2014).

The question that needs to be raised is: how can it be said that evangelicals can accept 'two-thirds' of the *Catechism* if this document speaks of the (Roman Catholic) church whenever it speaks of Christ, the Spirit and, by extension, the Trinity? Are we sure that the real difference between evangelicals and Catholics lies in ecclesiology, given that the Roman Catholic view of the church is argued for in Christological and pneumatological (i.e. related to the Holy Spirit) terms? Is the Christ of the *Catechism* the Jesus Christ of the Bible or the Christ of the Roman Church? Of course, there is a sense in which Rome confesses the historical Jesus Christ, as the Son of God become man. Yet, it is also true that Rome appeals to the same 'Christ' to support other doctrines and practices that are not biblical.

A similar problem can be seen with the US-based initiative Evangelicals and Catholics Together, whose 1994 founding document is referenced by Noll and Nystrom. In reading that text, one has the impression that there is significant doctrinal commonality between the two constituencies represented in the dialogue. However, as Jun Vencer (the then General Secretary of the World Evangelical Fellowship) has rightly pointed out in critically evaluating the document, 'the use of common language does not mean that the meanings are the same'.[7] In other words, the mere act of subscribing to a declaration is no indication of a genuinely recovered unity if each party attributes substantially different nuances to the agreed text. The only outcome of using the same words pretending they mean the same thing is to blur the meaning of the word 'Christian',[8] introducing ambiguity to a degree that becomes detrimental to true agreement.

Common viewpoint 2: This is a new era for evangelicals and Catholics

Another sentiment that is often expressed in the present-day ecumenical setting is along these lines: 'We are living in a new era; the

---

7   J. Vencer, 'Commentary on *ECT*', in H. Fuller, *People of the Mandate: The story of the World Evangelical Fellowship* (Carlisle: Paternoster; Grand Rapids, MI: Baker, 1996), pp. 191–193.

8   I. Murray, 'Evangelicals and Catholics Together: a movement of watershed significance?', *The Banner of Truth* 393 (1996), p. 12.

controversies of the past are over, and we should strive to reconcile Rome and the Protestant Reformation.' So, is it true that we are living in a 'new era'? To give an answer, we need to place this question in a wider historical and theological context, because otherwise we risk reducing everything to the here and now. This preliminary observation about method is always valid, but even more so when analysing Roman Catholicism, which is an institution that boasts a doctrinal, institutional and cultural heritage that spans two thousand years of history. Roman Catholicism has to be assessed using macro-categories able to hold together the largest possible number of elements. Failing to do this will lead to a collection of fragments, just pieces of Catholicism, which will not allow for a real understanding of its dimensions, depth, connections and projects. A 'spiritual' assessment cannot ignore the fact that while we are dealing with a system made up of people, they are in fact people within a framework that expresses itself in a history, a doctrine, a bond to the sacraments, a political commitment, a financial system, popular piety, a plurality of spiritual expressions and so on, all of which are nonetheless connected to an institutional centre and a theological heart. To speak of a 'new era' it is important to remember that throughout the course of its history Catholicism has known some particularly significant eras. Following is a brief summary.[9]

The era of imperial Catholicism

In the fourth century – between the Edict of Milan issued by the Roman emperor Constantine which granted religious freedom to all his subjects (AD 313) and the Edict of Thessalonika under Theodosius which proclaimed Christianity as the state religion (AD 380) – Catholicism quickly transformed itself into a religious empire, forged in the institutional mould of the empire and animated by an imperial ideology. From the ashes of the Roman Empire rose an imperial church that assumed a pyramidal institutional structure and clothed itself with Christian language and symbols. The imperial

---

9 An overview of the history of Roman Catholicism is provided by G. O'Collins and M. Farrugia, *Catholicism: The story of Catholic Christianity* (Oxford: Oxford University Press, 2014).

hubris of Roman Catholicism (that is, its desire to be both church and state) is its original sin – one which has never been seriously questioned, let alone refuted internally. The orthodoxy of primitive Christianity has been gradually broadened in the attempt to assimilate new beliefs and new practices, causing the Christian faith to become self-contradictory. The desire to represent all of humanity has moved the point of entry into the church from conversion to Christ to the baptism administered by the church, leading to the establishing of a church composed of baptized people and not of believers. Biblical revelation has in fact been relativized due to the growing role of the church's tradition. The church has become a nominal church made up of baptized people who are not necessarily believers. The grace of God has become the property of a religious institution that claims it can administer and dispense God's grace through its sacramental system. The imperial era gave rise to an imperial DNA that Catholicism has never laid aside. During this era, all biblical renewal movements were either fought against or assimilated through a policy of domestication to the imperial ideology. Niches of different forms of spirituality were carved out so as to be inoffensive and lifeless, and thus maintain the status quo.

The era of oppositional Catholicism

The second great age of the Catholic Church was that of the Counter-Reformation, structured around two central moments: the Council of Trent (1545–63) and the First Vatican Council (1869–70). The Roman Catholic Church's long trajectory is characterized by a doctrinal trend which is at the same time abrasive, dulling, and interested in affirming the centrality and superiority of the church. It is the age in which the modern Catholic doctrine based on the prerogative of the church as *alter Christus* (another Christ) is formed; it is the age in which the doctrine of the two sources of revelation is expressed: Scripture and Tradition; it is the age in which the church elevates itself to the point of thinking that its imperial structure is the divine will of God. Confronted with the Protestant Reformation, which invited the church to rid itself of its self-referentiality and rediscover the gospel of God's grace, Rome reacted with a strengthened sacramental system that explicitly positioned the church as the mediator of divine grace. Confronted with modernity, which pushed for a review of the prerogatives of the church over society and people's consciences, Rome elevated its main institution (the papacy) to an even more accentuated role, as well as dogmatizing some Marian beliefs without any biblical support whatsoever. This recovery of a robust identity also led to a missionary expansion of Catholicism and the development of mystical and Marian forms of spirituality.

The era of a compliant and captivating Catholicism

The model of the oppositional era led to isolation and a marginalized role for Roman Catholicism. A change took place with Vatican II (1962–5). Here a new era began, when instead of siding against the modern world, Rome changed strategy, choosing instead to assimilate modernity, to penetrate it from within without changing its own essence. Now Rome had adopted the method of 'updating': adjustment without structural reform, incorporation without loss or cost, expansion of the system without purification, development without renunciation of tradition, a continuous adding without subtracting anything. Reflecting on the outcomes of Vatican II, the Waldensian Italian theologian Vittorio Subilia has rightly spoken of the 'new catholicity of Catholicism', expressed as a different posture, a new style, a new language.[10] This updating takes place in every direction, however: in the direction of theological liberalism, making room for a critical reading of the Bible and universalism of salvation; in the evangelical direction, learning the linguistic code of evangelical spirituality (having a personal relationship with Christ, etc.); in the direction of Marian theology, traditionalism, ecumenism and so on. The result is a 360-degree expansionary catholicity, one that still maintains the sacramental, hierarchical, devotional and imperial structures (certainly made more discreet but definitely still present) – all of which revolve around an

---

10 V. Subilia, *La nuova cattolicità del cattolicesimo* (Turin: Claudiana, 1967).

abnormal and dilated ecclesiology and around the fundamental pillars of traditional doctrine.

The question for us

Without quoting its documents often, Pope Francis incarnates the catholicity of Vatican II: open to dialogue, merciful, pleasing, but without paying any dogmatic, theological or spiritual price. The imperial and Counter-Reformation framework of the former ages remains, only 'updated' to the new requirements of the contemporary global world. Francis speaks all languages – evangelical, ecumenical, interreligious, secular, charismatic, traditional. He seems to draw close to everyone without actually moving. He seems to reach out to everyone without going very far. And then, the fact that many people (from secularists to Muslims, and including liberal Protestants and evangelicals) consider him close to them must make us ask: is he really near to anyone? In other words, the strategy of the 'poly-hedron' seems to be the instrument of catholicity that has its roots in Vatican II and that fulfils it: all have to relate to a Roman church which has axes of various lengths in order to reach everyone but without shifting its centre of gravity. Rome has already reached such a well-oiled balance that it can play on more than one table at the same time without altering its overall framework.

In this climate, some people claim that the Reformation has practically finished because there no longer exists the oppositional Catholicism that rejected it. Catholicism has widened its synthesis and has also made room for the concerns of the Reformation, though trimmed of their groundbreaking character and bent to enable them to coexist, to cohabit, to live side by side with other demands opposed to the gospel within a Catholic system which is evermore eclectic and plural but still Roman and papal. Catholicism continues to add places to the table and extend the menu; it variegates more and more the codes of its behaviour, working to fulfil its vocation to unite the world inside the net of catholicity and under the effective or honorary jurisdiction of a supreme head.

In this new era of captivating catholicity there will be an open welcome to those evangelicals who have made peace with the imperial structures of the Church of Rome and its abnormal theology, and who are no longer concerned about a comprehensive reform in accordance with the gospel. These evangelicals instead are content to be able to integrate their own spirituality into a system that is more fluid but still vertebrate, that is programmatically open to everything and yet opposed to everything. The criterion of the system is not the gospel of Christ (although the words of the gospel are disseminated here and there) but a version of the gospel that guarantees the universalist and Rome-centred strategy of Roman Catholicism. The words are similar, yet the world is different.

This new era for evangelicals and Catholics requires us to ask a question which is both old and relevant for every generation of believers: can the Church of Rome be renewed in accordance with the gospel from within, or do we have to envisage moving past it and leaving it behind in the name of the gospel? With its encumbrance of unreformable dogmas, imperial institutions, projects of omnivorous catholicity, can the Church of Rome be touched by the gospel in its propulsive heart? In other words: is the gospel just one option among many possibilities, or is it the radical 'yes' to the Word of God that says 'no' to all forms of idolatry? Can a church, whichever one it is, be programmatically open to a multitude of offers, or, if it wants to be a church, must it be founded exclusively on the biblical gospel?

So, are we entering a new era with regard to the relationship between evangelicals and Catholics? A long look at history, the spiritual discernment of the gospel and the overall view of the Spirit leads us to answer both 'yes' and 'no'. Certainly, with Vatican II a different period began which needs to be understood. It is wrong to have a flattened or static view of Roman Catholicism. Nevertheless, Vatican II and Pope Francis, who is its most successful incarnation, are only the latest evolutionary step in a system that was born and developed with an 'original sin' from which it has not yet been redeemed but which instead has been consolidated. No ecumenical diplomacy will be able to change it and neither will the addition of a new evangelical offer to the traditional menu of Roman Catholicism. The invitation of the Lord Jesus applies to everyone: 'The time is fulfilled, and the kingdom of God is at hand; repent and believe in the gospel' (Mark 1:15). The real new era, God willing, will be when Roman Catholicism breaks the imperial ecclesiological pattern and reforms its own catholicity, basing it no longer on its assimilation project but on faithfulness to the gospel.[11]

Common viewpoint 3: We have a common Nicene Christianity

There is a third approach that is often used in arguing for the rapprochement between evangelicals and Catholics. This time the connection comes from church history and, specifically, from the heritage of the first centuries of the church. The terms 'Nicene faith' or 'Nicene Christianity' are considered synonyms of Christianity. They are sufficiently defined in the essentials, but still free from the subsequent confessional incrustations that 'divided' Christianity between the Eastern and Western churches in the eleventh century and the Roman Catholic and Protestant churches in the sixteenth century.

Wanting to commend the plausibility of the Christian faith, in 1952 the British intellectual C. S. Lewis coined the expression 'mere Christianity'.[12] He did so precisely to indicate those essential contours of the Christian faith that are enunciated in the Nicene Creed, which all Christians, whatever tradition they belong to (Roman Catholic, Protestant, Orthodox, etc.), make their own. In contemporary ecumenical theology, the 'Nicene faith', often referred to as the 'Great Tradition', is considered the theological platform on which all traditional Christian families must recognize one another

---

11 For an attempt to provide a brief yet solid evangelical analysis of Roman Catholicism, see for example 'An evangelical approach towards understanding Roman Catholicism', *Evangelicals Now* (December 2000), pp. 12–13; also in *European Journal of Theology* 10.1 (2001), pp. 32–35. The document was issued by the Italian Evangelical Alliance and published in several languages: Italian: 'Orientamenti evangelici per pensare il cattolicesimo', *Ideaitalia* 3.5 (1999), pp. 7–8; French: 'Le Catholicisme romain: une approche évangélique', *Vivre* 8–9 (2000), pp. 10–14, and *Fac-Réflexion* 51–52 (2000/2–3), pp. 44–49; German: 'Ein evangelikaler Ansatz zum Verständnis des Römischen Katholizismus', *Bibel Info* 59.3 (2001), pp. 10–13.
12 C. S. Lewis, *Mere Christianity* (London: Geoffrey Bles, 1952).

since they all stem from the historical tree of Nicene Christianity. In this perspective, Nicaea is a symbol of the undivided past that becomes the hope of a unity to be rediscovered.[13]

The appeal to Nicene Christianity in evangelicalism

The strong appeal to the 'Nicene faith' goes beyond ecumenical circles. Wanting to overcome the fundamentalist tendency that has downplayed the historical heritage of the faith, important sectors of the evangelical world have loudly called on evangelicalism to 'reclaim' the apostolic testimony that finds its dogmatic symbol par excellence in the Nicene faith.[14] This pressing invitation has set in motion a certain dynamism in the study of the Church Fathers in the last few decades, even among evangelical scholars.[15] The idea has gained popularity among evangelicals that the Nicene faith (centred on the profession of the Trinity and on an orthodox Christology) is the common ground between evangelicals and Roman Catholics, while differences would lie in doctrines such as soteriology, ecclesiology and Mariology.[16] The Nicene faith apparently shared by all is the common basis that would reflect 'a deeper agreement' between all the expressions of Christianity, 'despite profound disagreements' between them that occurred later.[17] In the words of Craig Carter:

> The Great Tradition of Christian orthodoxy begins with the Old and New Testaments, crystalizes in the fourth-century trinitarian debates, and then continues through Augustine, Thomas Aquinas, the leading Protestant Reformers, post-Reformation scholasticism, and contemporary conservative

---

13 See e.g. C. Steitz (ed.), *Nicene Christianity: The future of a new ecumenism* (Grand Rapids, MI: Brazos Press, 2004).

14 T. George (ed.), *Evangelicals and the Nicene Faith: Reclaiming the apostolic witness* (Grand Rapids, MI: Baker, 2011).

15 For a survey see K. Stewart, 'Evangelicalism and patristic Christianity: 1517 to the present', *Evangelical Quarterly* 80.4 (2008), pp. 307–321.

16 This is the approach taken by the Evangelicals and Catholics Together initiative since 1994.

17 As is argued by K. Collins and J. Walls, *Roman but Not Catholic: What remains at stake 500 years after the Reformation* (Grand Rapids, MI: Baker, 2017), p. 78.

Roman Catholic, Eastern Orthodox, and Protestant confessional theology.[18]

Here is the 'Nicene' ecumenism of the Great Tradition: a transversal front that embraces the conservatives of all the families of Christendom and that incorporates all those who refer to Nicaea as their theological platform.

The question to ask is whether or not the Nicene faith can play the role that is assigned to it. One needs to verify the plausibility of the idea that contemporary ecumenism can find in Nicaea a meeting point that historically precedes the confessional controversies, theologically welcomes all the confessions developed after Nicaea and provides an ecumenical common basis for rebuilding the lost unity. So, is the Nicene faith (or can it be) the theological basis for contemporary ecumenism? The answer is negative for at least three reasons. Let's look at them in order.

Three objections to the ecumenical use of the Nicene faith

First, the vocabulary of Nicaea to which all confessions refer is the same: 'God the Father', 'Jesus Christ', 'salvation', 'Holy Spirit', 'virgin Mary', 'church', 'a holy apostolic catholic church', 'baptism', 'remission of sins'. But while the signifiers are the same, inasmuch as the same sounds combine to form the same words linked together in the same order, this cannot be said of the theological meaning of the words used. When a Roman Catholic refers to the 'virgin Mary', to 'salvation', to 'the church' and so on, does he or she mean the same thing as an evangelical, an Eastern Orthodox or a liberal Protestant would mean when using the same words? Of course not. Think of the word 'salvation': a Roman Catholic would understand it as a sacramental journey under the authority of the church and with the help of the intercessions of Mary and the saints; an evangelical understands salvation as being grounded solely on Jesus Christ and

---

18 C. A. Carter, *Interpreting Scripture with the Great Tradition: Recovering the genius of premodern exegesis* (Grand Rapids, MI: Baker, 2018), p. xi.

received by faith alone; a liberal would tend to understand it as the attempt to be a better person living in a better society.

The words are the same but their meanings substantially different.

Reference to Nicaea cannot bridge the gap. Consider the word 'church': the Roman Catholic has a view of the church as a hierarchical society whose absolute leader is the pope, who is given the title of 'Vicar of Christ'; evangelicals understand the church largely as a fellowship of believers who bear witness to the gospel but who do not prolong the incarnation of Jesus Christ and therefore do not reclaim his prerogatives. The 'Great Tradition' speaks of the 'church', but do we believe in the same 'church'? Examples could be easily multiplied.

There is an area of overlap and an area of differentiation that makes the use of the same terms equivocal. In fact, the words of the Nicene Creed are marked by theologically different understandings. In the common recitation, the impression is that they all say the same thing; this is true on a phonetic level, but not at the semantic level. Calling the Nicene faith the common basis can be an emotional appeal, but it is not a responsible action because, while the impression is given that we say the same things, the reality is that we are saying *different* things.

Second, Nicaea is not a point of arrival, but a step in the history of the church. For example, Nicaea was followed by the Council of Ephesus (AD 431), which dogmatized the Marian title of 'Mother of God'; the Council of Trent (1545–63), which defined justification as a synergistic process within a sacramental system; the Marian dogmas of the immaculate conception (1854) and bodily assumption (1950); the First Vatican Council (1869–70) with the dogma of papal infallibility; and by Vatican II (1962–5) with its inclusive catholicity. The theology of the various traditions is today characterized by a doctrinal and spiritual stratification that is irreversible and no longer that of Nicaea. For example, Roman Catholicism has given dogmatic status to its Mariology and to the papacy. These Marian and papal dogmas impinge on Christology, the doctrine of the Spirit, ecclesiology and salvation. When Nicaea refers to Jesus Christ, the Spirit and the church, present-day Roman Catholicism also reads Mary into the background. When Nicaea refers to salvation and the forgiveness of sins, Roman Catholicism after Trent reads the sacraments and indulgences. It is not possible to put the clock back as if seventeen hundred years of history had not happened. It is simplistic, as well as antihistoric, to think that the common profession of Nicaea can be extracted from the important additions which have become the Roman Catholic interpretative keys of creedal Christianity. Nicaea cannot ultimately bring us together because evangelicals and Catholics have developed different dogmas and practices in their histories in all key areas of the Christian faith. We are talking about different things, using the same words to describe radically different worlds.

Third and finally, the Nicene faith cannot be the basis of contemporary ecumenism because of the different role that the different Christian traditions ascribe to the profession of a creed. What does it mean to 'profess' a creed like that of Nicaea? To learn it by heart and recite it? To believe in the affirmations it contains? To identify oneself in the world view to which it gives voice? To perform a conventional act linked to a traditional religious practice? To mechanically repeat a 'jingle' that evokes our childhood? The range of possibilities for the appropriation of Nicaea is wide. For example, how many liberal Christians (who would have no problem saying that Nicaea is important) believe that God is truly the creator of the heavens and the earth? How convinced are they that Jesus was really born of the virgin Mary, or that he bodily rose from the dead? If we have even a little acquaintance with contemporary theology, we will realize how many interpretations there are of these and other cornerstones of the Christian faith. So what does it mean to profess the united faith in a united way if, despite reciting the same words, we believe substantially different doctrines? In addition, for how many nominal Christians does the recitation of the creed make a difference in their lives? What does it mean to say 'I believe . . .' for many people who, despite having been baptized and occasionally attending religious services, are not regenerated and therefore are not believers? Of course they can recite the Nicene Creed, but this profession is very often a rhetorical exercise with almost no spiritual value. Reciting it together does not in and of itself bring unity.

Referring to Nicaea as the common basis of ecumenism is wishful thinking rather than theologically responsible hope. In the light of these three reasons, among Christian confessions and traditions there is a deeper disagreement, despite some areas of apparent and formal agreement. The way of unity always passes by the biblical truth that the Council of Nicaea tried to honour, even in the complexities of history. In itself, Nicaea is necessary. But it is not sufficient to express the biblical unity which the Lord Jesus prayed for and gave his life to achieve.

Common viewpoint 4: What unites us is greater than what divides us

The fourth common view is a particularly popular one. Many people readily recognize the differences between evangelicals and Catholics (they are so evident!), but they are also impressed by what seems to unite them: they read the Scriptures, they invoke the Trinity, they believe in the historical Jesus, they have a sense of sin and the need for salvation, they believe in the afterlife and so on.

One recent restatement of such a position comes from the already cited book by North American evangelical scholars Ken Collins and Jim Walls.[19] The authors present in a masterly fashion the convincing case that Rome's catholicity is not catholic enough. It is too tied to the Roman geography, power structure and imperial ideology to be truly catholic. According to them, Roman Catholicism is more Roman than Catholic; indeed it is Roman and not catholic! This is a bold statement, ecumenically non-correct, yet hard to push back against! Having said that, Collins and Walls do not go far enough in coming to terms with the consequences of what they so convincingly showcase. They still operate with the mindset according to which 'what divides evangelicals and the Roman Catholic Church is less than what unites them'. Here is the way they put it: 'Deep

---

19 Collins and Walls, *Roman but Not Catholic*.

Disagreement despite Deeper Agreement'.[20] According to them, the deeper agreement is (not surprisingly) the trinitarian and Christological foundation of the 'catholic' tradition (as it is enshrined in the early creeds of the ancient church), whereas the deep disagreement refers to the later Roman accretions (as they are, for example, reflected in the papacy).

This way of understanding the dividing line between evangelicals and Catholics is popular in ecumenical circles, but it is not fully consistent with the thesis endorsed by the authors. The fact that the Roman Catholic Church is committed to its Roman identity and to its catholic heritage means that even the catholic (i.e. trinitarian and Christological) core is affected by its Roman commitment. According to the Catholic Church, the Roman and non-biblical elements (i.e. the Roman pontiff, the Roman imperial institutions, the Roman hierarchical ecclesiology) are not accidents of history; they are considered to be *de jure divino* (i.e. stemming from divine law, being rooted in God's will) constitutive components of the church. For Rome, its catholic and Roman dual identity is grounded in the divine will. So these foundational Roman commitments do affect the way in which the 'catholic' ones are understood and articulated in doctrine and practice. The 'catholic' heritage of Rome has been shaped, curved and bent by its Roman additions to the point where it is no longer the way it was in the ancient church. It is a different catholicity. It is Roman Catholicism. Moreover, all of the spurious Roman elements are argued for in trinitarian and Christological ways by Roman Catholic theology. For example, the pope is believed to be the 'vicar' of Christ and chosen by the Holy Spirit. This is a trinitarian argument, but a kind of trinitarianism that is significantly different from the biblical one to the point of allowing and demanding the wrong Roman developments. Here we can see the complexity of Roman Catholic dogma as it intersects with what might otherwise be 'mere' Christian belief.

---

20 Collins and Walls, *Roman but Not Catholic*, p. 78.

Mariology superseding Christology?

Roman Catholic Mariology provides another area where important trinitarian relations are wrongly articulated, thus making it possible to question the orthodoxy of Roman Catholic trinitarian theology.[21] Since the dogmatic pronouncement of the Council of Ephesus in AD 431 (when Mary was given the title of 'Mother of God'), the Mariological trajectory has been strongly pushed forward in ever-expanding and almost self-referential terms. After Ephesus, the veneration of Mary became prominent in devotional practices, doxological patterns and the religious arts. Christianity went through a Marian shift in terms of liturgy and general orientation. The paradox was that the council that wanted to reaffirm the full deity and humanity of Jesus ended up promoting a functional heresy. Individuals, groups and movements began to develop quasi-obsessive Marian interpretations of the Christian faith, and Mary became the figure most prayed to in daily life. She was not meant to divert attention from her Son, but her post-Ephesus perception functionally superseded him in terms of experiential forms of Christianity.

The Son always depicted in the company of the Mother, the Mother often portrayed as bigger than the (baby) Son, coupled with a growing prayer investment directed towards her, contributed to the gradual reconfiguration of Christian spirituality *away* from Christ (who began to be seen as too distant, too divine, too remote to be approached) and *towards* Mary with her maternal, tender and compassionate attitude. Christ's humanity – which is essential in recognizing his role as a mediator connecting the incarnate Son with us creatures – was progressively rarefied at the expense of his divinity. Christ's divinity was eventually pushed to the forefront, making him too far above to be invoked directly.

The balance of the confession in the early creeds of Jesus Christ being 'fully God, fully man' was nominally maintained but practically abandoned by the increasingly Marian spirituality of the

---

21 At this point I re-present parts of a chapter of my book *A Christian's Pocket Guide to Mary: Mother of God?* (Fearn: Christian Focus, 2017), pp. 83–87.

post-Ephesus church. The vacuum left by the lack of appreciation for the humanity of Christ was filled by the growth of the role of Mary the Mother. The nearness of the Mother of God was the answer to the remoteness of the Son of God and even caused the Son to be perceived further as being too distant to understand and take care of people in the struggles of life. In other words, perhaps unintentionally, the Mother swallowed the Son. Orthodox Christology based on the councils of Nicaea (AD 325) and Chalcedon (AD 451) continued to be formally professed and defended; in reality, the appropriation of these Christological truths became a far too abstract discourse and of little spiritual benefit. What was practised at the popular doxological level was an all-embracing Mariology that accounted for the spiritual needs of the people and whetted further theological development along Mariological lines.

Mariology obscuring the work of the Spirit?

There is more than the above. In trinitarian relationships, the work of the Son is strictly connected with that of the Holy Spirit. According to the Bible, the Son's role as mediator is worked out by and through the Spirit. For example, it is the Spirit who helps us in our weakness by interceding for us in accordance with God's will (Rom. 8:26–27). Christ is the mediator to the Father, and the Spirit enables us to come to him. What happened with the unchecked rise of Mariology? By pushing Christ's humanity outside the picture and filling the void with the intercessions of the Mother of God, Mariological development diminished also the role of the Holy Spirit by not recognizing his vital involvement in the mediatorial work of the Son. In becoming the figure nearer to the Son who could always be invoked and who was felt closer than the Son, Mary practically unravelled the bond between the Son and the Spirit and undermined the relationship between the faithful and the Spirit. The 'gain' of Mariology was the 'loss' of the Holy Spirit. The impressive growth of Mariology meant the disturbing disappearance of the Spirit.

Marianism, then, obscured the nearness of the Son and froze the unique contribution of the Spirit. Beyond excesses in devotional practices – which are nonetheless intrinsically related to the nature of Mariology itself – the Roman Catholic view of Mary poses serious questions at the level of its trinitarian implications. Formal adherence to the creedal basis of the person and work of Jesus Christ needs to be matched with a coherent spirituality centred on the praise of the triune God – Father, Son and Holy Spirit – something that does not happen in Mariology because of its inflated view of Mary and its consequent marginalization of Christ and the Spirit. In spite of the stated intention not to divert attention from the Son, Mariology tends to be an intruder into trinitarian harmony and an obstacle to a full appreciation of who the triune God is and what he has done for us.

Back to the 'what unites us is greater than what divides us' argument. The point is that the 'deep disagreements despite deeper agreement' approach adopted in the book by Collins and Walls should actually be reversed. Between the evangelical faith and Rome are deep agreements despite *deeper disagreements*. Agreements lie in the phonetic use of common words and the residual biblical meaning in Catholic terms. Disagreements lie in the basic structure of the respective theologies: the Roman Catholic world being built around multiple foundations other than the Bible. Even doctrines like the Trinity and Christology have been infected by the way the Roman Catholic system works, and the way they are worked out in theology and practice is linked organically to the Roman Catholic frame of reference.

Common viewpoint 5: The rise of Evangelical Catholicism is encouraging

'The beginning of wisdom is the definition of words' is a statement attributed to Socrates. If you define a word in a certain way, you make claims about reality. Our postmodern culture has encouraged us to come to terms with the fact that words do not have stable meanings but exist in a flux that drives them in one way or another depending on the interests of their users. This is the current situation for the word 'evangelical'.

There was a time when the word 'evangelical' meant something like the following. Biblically, it was defined around the evangel (i.e. the gospel) as it is truly witnessed in Scripture. Historically, it has referred to the sixteenth-century Protestant Reformation and the evangelical revivals of subsequent centuries. Doctrinally, it has pointed to Christian orthodoxy, focusing on the formal principle of biblical authority (*sola scriptura*) and the material principle of justification by faith alone (*sola gratia* and *sola fide*). Experientially, it has majored on the need for personal conversion resulting in a transformed life. Religiously, it has distinguished itself from (and was often opposed to) Roman Catholicism, Eastern Orthodoxy and liberalism. From John Wycliffe (*doctor evangelicus*) to Carl Henry, from Martin Luther to Charles Spurgeon, from Pietism to the Lausanne Movement, there has been a loosely defined yet shared meaning of the word which was also accepted by non-evangelicals. It is true that evangelicals have always discussed the minutiae of what 'evangelical' really means, of its ins and outs. There are entire bookshelves that are dedicated to these important, at times fierce, debates. Yet the word has retained a rather stable meaning that has fostered common identity and a sense of belonging, describing a 'Christian family' throughout the centuries and in our global world.[22] We are now witnessing a new attempt to get a handle on the word 'evangelical' in order to give it an altogether different meaning.

Evangelical Catholicism and the current genetic modification

The recent book by George Weigel on Evangelical Catholicism[23] is a clever attempt to re-engineer the word 'evangelical' by overlooking its biblical focus, by severing its historical roots and replacing them with other roots, by changing its doctrinal outlook, by staffing its experiential ethos differently and by renegotiating its religious use. In other words, this is a genetic modification of a word.

---

22 See the classic book by D. W. Bebbington, *Evangelicalism in Modern Britain: A history from the 1730s to the 1980s* (London: Unwin Hyman, 1989).
23 G. Weigel, *Evangelical Catholicism: Deep reform in the 21st-century church* (New York, NY: Basic Books, 2013).

The basic thesis of the book is that Evangelical Catholicism (EC) is a qualifier of present-day Roman Catholicism as it stemmed from the magisterium of Pope Leo XIII (1878–1903), was expounded by Vatican II (1962–5), found its champion in John Paul II (1978–2005) and was again reinforced by Benedict XVI (2005–13). It is a new account of the word 'Evangelical'. Whereas previous scholarship referred to this time in Catholic history as marked by 'ressourcement' (i.e. reappropriation of sources: Scripture and Tradition) and 'aggiornamento' (i.e. update of approach, not of doctrine), Weigel calls it 'Evangelical' Catholicism.

According to Weigel, 'Evangelical' is a qualifying adjective, not a noun. The noun that carries 'thick' meaning in this phrase is 'Catholicism'. Curiously, what used to be termed as 'Roman Catholicism' is now shortened to 'Catholicism' alone. All the Roman elements of Roman Catholicism are nonetheless part of this new construct known as Evangelical Catholicism: sacraments, Mariology, hierarchy, traditions, papacy, devotions and so on. To this 'Catholicism' Weigel adds the adjective 'Evangelical', which basically refers to the depth of convictions and the passion to make them known. Evangelical Catholicism is a full-orbed Roman Catholicism practised with strong impetus and missionary zeal. Catholicism is the doctrinal and institutional hardware, while 'Evangelical' is the sociological and psychological software. While doctrine remains deeply Roman Catholic, the spiritual mood is called 'Evangelical'.

The tip of the iceberg

The major genetic modification surrounding the word 'evangelical' is just the tip of the iceberg of a bigger plan. The whole book mirrors the continuing attempt to change the meaning of words that have historically belonged to the evangelical vocabulary, such as 'conversion', 'evangelization' and 'mission'. Take 'conversion', for example. It used to be a catchword for evangelical witness. Evangelicals used it in pointing out the time when they were 'not' converted and the time when they 'got' converted and believed. According to the book *Evangelical Catholicism*, 'conversion' is a continual process instead of a once-and-for-all experience. We stand in permanent need of being converted, and that fits the 'sacramental' Roman Catholic view of the Christian life whereby we depend on the sacraments of the church from beginning to end. Evangelical Catholicism deconstructs the evangelical meaning of the word 'conversion' and reconstructs it by saying that it is a lifelong process which fully occurs in the sacramental system of the Roman Catholic Church. We use the same word but mean different things.

Evangelicals may think that Evangelical Catholicism is evangelical in the historical and theological sense, but it is not. It is Roman Catholicism that takes the sociological and psychological 'evangelical' zeal and embodies it in the traditional Roman Catholic faith. Evangelical Catholicism can perhaps be seen as a brain transplant of the word 'evangelical' and is aimed at radically reprogramming it. It implies that the old use could not stand on its own and that it makes sense only if it is attached to Roman Catholicism. Of course, we operate in a free-market world of words and it is perfectly legitimate for pressure groups to try to change the meaning of words. Nobody can claim words to be personal property, but everybody should be concerned when such a radically revisionist plan is put into action.

We started this section quoting Socrates and we will now end it with a reference to Virgil. In the *Aeneid*, we are told how the Greeks captured the city of Troy after a long but fruitless siege. The story of the Trojan horse tells us how what seemed to be a victory turned out to be a devastating defeat. Evangelical Catholicism may appear as an evangelically friendly project that we may want to welcome in. In actual fact, however, it is an intellectually courageous attempt to redefine what 'Evangelical' means, maintaining the same spelling but giving it a Roman Catholic meaning. It is a different world altogether.

Common viewpoint 6: The Church of Rome is becoming Protestant

The recent commemoration of the Reformation (in Lund, Sweden, on 31 October 2016) is only the tip of the iceberg in Pope Francis's ecumenical efforts.[24] His relentless activity in meeting Christian leaders (from the patriarchs of Constantinople and Moscow to mainstream Protestant denominational leaders and several Pentecostal pastors) is a qualifying mark of his pontificate that raises growing concerns inside the Catholic Church too. His constant remarks about the need to speed the way towards unity appear to soften, if not downplay, the traditional conditions for such unity according to Rome. Some Catholic critics are worried that the pope seems to spend more time with non-Catholics than with people of his own church. This was particularly apparent after his recent verbal appreciation of Martin Luther in an interview given to the Italian Catholic newspaper *Avvenire*, where the blunt question was asked: is the pope making the Catholic Church Protestant?[25]

In step with Vatican II

In the Western church, talks about reform have been going on since the councils of Vienne (1312), Constance (1414–18) and Lateran V (1512–17). The word 'reform' is therefore part of the language of the church, and was common even before the Protestant Reformation. The Council of Trent (1545–63) used it abundantly to promote changes at the level of ecclesiastical organization. In subsequent centuries the word was treated with caution, if not suspicion, given its Protestant flavour. It was Vatican II (1962–5) that began to circulate it (e.g. *LG* 4), also using 'aggiornamento' (updating) and 'renewal'. Typically, the Catholic sense of reformation is continuity in change and change in continuity. Again, it is Vatican II that sets the tone for interpretation when it says that 'every renewal of the Church is essentially grounded in an increase of fidelity to her own calling' (*UR* 6). In reforming itself, the Roman Catholic Church does not lose anything of the past but rather tries to become more faithful to what it is already. The criterion of reformation is not external and objective, as would be the case with recognizing it in the Word of

---

24 For an evangelical evaluation of Pope Francis see my free ebook, *Papa Francisco en perspectiva evangélica* (2017): <www.reformandainitiative.org/resources/ebook-gratuito-papa-francisco-en-perspectiva-evangelica-leonardo-de-chirico>.

25 <https://www.avvenire.it/papa/pagine/giubileo-ecumenismo-concilio-intervista-esclusiva-del-papa-ad-avvenire>.

God, but always internal and ecclesial, that is, the church itself setting the parameters for its own renewal.

In the interview given to *Avvenire*, Pope Francis rejects the view according to which commemorating the Protestant Reformation was an unwarranted 'forward flight'. He then defends his actions by referring to Vatican II as the framework for his ecumenical initiatives. This is no surprise. Vatican II (1962–5) sought to re-orientate the ecumenical direction of the Roman Catholic Church by recognizing signs of the true church in other communities and by calling non-Catholics 'separated brethren'.[26] One of the goals of the council was to encourage full unity among Christian churches and communities, all reconciled with the theological outlook and ecclesiastical structures of the Roman Church. There is nothing new under the sun. What Francis is doing in the sphere of ecumenism was all prepared by and previewed at Vatican II. Each pontiff in his own way – John XXII, Paul VI, John Paul II and Benedict XVI – has tried to implement the ecumenical thrust of the council. Francis confirms himself as the pope who, without necessarily quoting the documents of Vatican II at length, perhaps embodies its 'spirit' more than his predecessors.

More specifically, Francis makes reference to the fifty-year-old dialogue between the Roman Catholic Church and the Lutherans which culminated in the 1999 *Joint Declaration* on justification signed under John Paul II and under the leadership of then Cardinal Ratzinger. For Francis this document settles the main theological issues raised by the Reformation, paving the way for even fuller unity. After this landmark agreement, nothing of significance is left of the Reformation apart from the regretful political attachments of self-referential churches that are entrenched in their past.

Parameters of unity

The pope rejects the idea that he is making his church more Protestant and appeals to Vatican II as the large theological canvas on

---

26 For an evangelical assessment of Vatican II see my 'El Vaticano II, banco de pruebas de la teología evangélica', in *Soli Deo gloria: aspectos y legado del pensamiento evangélico de José Grau* (Ciudad Real: Editorial Pelegrino, 2016), pp. 115–155.

which the *Joint Declaration* represents a new ecumenical landscape. He sees himself as standing at a point on a long-term trajectory towards unity. Moreover, the fact that he approaches other Christian traditions and communities (e.g. the different bodies of Eastern Orthodoxy) with similar if not more intensive fervour indicates that he is not particularly attracted to Protestantism only. His ecumenical zeal goes even beyond the borders of Christianity and spills over to the world of other religions and the secular world. He takes unity, that is, Christian unity, as part of a larger goal that has to do with the unity of humankind.

Returning to the question about the Protestantization of the Catholic Church, there is a major argument running through Pope Francis's assessment of the Reformation in the context of his ardent desire for unity. His interpretation of the history of the Reformation and its continuing significance de facto eliminates theology from the picture and replaces the driving force of unity with actions like doing things together and praying together. In other words, 'Scripture alone' (the Bible has supreme authority over the church), 'faith alone' (salvation is a gift received by believing in Christ and trusting him) and 'Christ alone' (the whole Christian life is centred on him) are nothing but relics of a distant past. According to the pope, the Roman Catholic Church has already absorbed these concerns, and those who want to continue to wave the Reformation flag are seen as wanting to continue a power game based on church politics. Is this really the case? Of course not. Certainly the Reformation had political overtones. However, as the recent statement *Is the Reformation Over?*[27] – signed by dozens of evangelical theologians and leaders worldwide – argues:

> In all its varieties and at times conflicting tendencies, the Protestant Reformation was ultimately a call to (1) recover the authority of the Bible over the church and (2) appreciate afresh the fact that salvation comes to us through faith alone.

---

27 See Appendix 1.

30

These are standing and unresolved issues in the present-day relationship between Roman Catholics and evangelical Christians. Church politics, although inextricably interwoven, was not the main reason and is not the main legacy of the Reformation.

With Pope Francis the Roman Catholic Church is not becoming Reformed in the Protestant sense. It is simply becoming more 'catholic', that is, embracing and absorbing all, without losing its identity as 'Roman'. It is still embedded in the theological and institutional outlook that the Protestant Reformation called to renewal according to the gospel. The word 'reform' is used, but the world which gives meaning to it does not indicate a biblical reformation.

2

Key Roman Catholic word contexts: exploring the doctrinal field

Words do not live in isolation. They have their own specific connotation, but part of their meaning comes from the way they are connected to one another. When linked together they are part of a bigger whole that influences the way people and institutions understand them. The same is true for words related to faith. A theological word is not a self-contained unit. Though it carries its own semantic weight, it is also defined by when and where it is found, the web of references which are associated with it, who is involved in enacting it, and the practices that precede, accompany and follow it.

In this chapter particular attention will be given to some words or clusters of words which are significant in the Christian faith. Although the terms are part of the vocabulary of all Christians, it is the particular Roman Catholic meaning that will be underlined and assessed here. If these theological words are approached superficially and atomistically, one may get the impression that they belong to the same deposit of the Christian faith shared by all who claim some kind of allegiance to it. A closer look will reveal that, beyond some commonality, they also carry significant differences which, taken as a whole, form another 'world' – one that is different from the world of the biblical faith.

Revelation and the Bible

'Revelation' is a word that is common between Roman Catholics and evangelical Protestants. The yardstick of biblical data sees the faith as being given to the saints once and for all time (Jude 3). Divine revelation has been made known in Christ once and for all, in the sense of its completeness (Heb. 1:1–2). It has certainly undergone a historical progression in the unfolding of salvation history, but in the fullness of time has reached its final apex in the mission of the Son of God (Gal. 4:4). After Christ, who is the culmination of revelation, no further revelation with equal authority to that of Scripture can be expected until his return. It is all recorded in the inspired books of the Bible, and the Word of God written is perfectly sufficient for teaching, reproof, correction and training in righteousness (2 Tim. 3:16). After the revelation of the Christ of the Bible, there can no longer be revelations but only interpretations of the already given revelation.[1]

The Roman Catholic perspective, while attributing a conclusive character to the revelation of Jesus Christ and to the Bible, has a wider understanding of revelation. Revelation is one 'divine wellspring' (*DV* 9) from which the Bible and tradition flow. The two means of transmission refer to the unique revelation that is interpreted authentically and authoritatively by the magisterium, that is, the official teaching of the Roman Catholic Church. What needs to be stressed here is that the stream of revelation by tradition can be extrabiblical and at times antibiblical. The example of the promulgation of the dogma of the assumption of Mary (1950), explicitly lacking any biblical warrant but well attested in tradition, indicates that such an idea is not just hypothetical. This dogma (i.e. binding belief for all Catholics) is that Mary, soon after dying, was taken body and soul to the glory of heaven. Where in Scripture is this revealed? Nowhere! But it is part of the Catholic tradition, and this tradition is the ground of what Rome teaches.

Where does authority lie?

The Roman Catholic understanding of revelation values Scripture to a certain extent, but it also values its own tradition(s) at the same time. The Bible is just one of the authorities but is not the only one,

---

1 See the standard evangelical work by C. F. H. Henry, *God, Revelation and Authority*, 6 vols. (Waco, TX: Word, 1976).

nor is it the highest. In Roman Catholic doctrine, God's revelation comes to us in the form of an oral tradition that takes two forms: the written voice found in the text of the Bible and the living voice of the official teaching of the Roman Catholic Church. According to this view, tradition is prior to the Bible, bigger than the Bible, and its present-day voice is not the biblical text but the continuing teaching of the church on whatever it advocates. In a telling passage, Vatican II affirms:

> it is not from Sacred Scripture alone that the Church draws her certainty about everything which has been revealed. Therefore both sacred tradition and Sacred Scripture are to be accepted and venerated with the same sense of loyalty and reverence. (*DV* 9)

The Bible, therefore, cannot be the ultimate authority. It cannot teach, reprove, correct and train if it is not the final word. There is something bigger than it and there is something more relevant than it, and this is the tradition that the Catholic Church gives voice to. According to Roman Catholicism the Bible is important but inconclusive. It is one form of revelation but not the final one. The word 'revelation' is the 'same' as the Protestant term, but its meaning and implications for Rome are massively different.

The Bible contains the Word

In a more recent papal document on the Word of God, the 2010 post-synodical exhortation *Verbum Domini* (*VD*),[2] Pope Benedict XVI reiterates mainstream Roman Catholic teaching on the relationship between divine revelation and the Bible. To start with, *VD* claims that the Word of God 'precedes and exceeds sacred Scripture, nonetheless Scripture, as inspired by God, contains the divine word' (17). *VD* claims that the Bible is the Word of God in the sense that it

---

2 <http://w2.vatican.va/content/benedict-xvi/en/apost_exhortations/documents/hf_ben-xvi_exh_20100930_verbum-domini.html>. Quotations from this document, and from other official documents issued by the Roman Catholic Church, will be referenced in the main body of the text by indicating the paragraph number.

contains the Word. There is the Bible and there is also a further word beyond the Bible that makes the Bible not sufficient on its own. What is at stake here is not the divine inspiration of the Bible (which *VD* firmly affirms) but the *sufficiency* of the Bible and its *finality*. For Pope Benedict, the Bible is the Word of God in some sense, but the Word of God is bigger than the Bible. The latter contains the former.

For Protestant readers especially, a comment is necessary on this point. Liberal theology has developed its own theology of the Word whereby the relationship between the Word and the Bible is thought of in dialectical and existential ways. In other words, for some versions of liberal theology, the Bible is a (fallible) testimony to the Word and it becomes the Word of God, if it ever becomes so, when the Spirit speaks through it. Now, the Roman Catholic version of the Word–Bible relationship is articulated in a different way. The premise is the same (i.e. the Bible *contains* the Word), but the outworking of the Word comes through the tradition of the Roman Catholic Church. The gap between the Word and the Bible is not existential but ecclesial. The church is the cradle of the Word, both in its past and written form (the Bible) and in its continuing utterances (Tradition). In this respect, Benedict XVI writes:

> The Church lives in the certainty that her Lord, who spoke in the past, continues today to communicate his word in her living Tradition and in sacred Scripture. Indeed, the word of God given to us in sacred Scripture as an inspired testimony to revelation; together with the Church's living Tradition, it constitutes the supreme rule of faith.
> (*VD* 18)

The Bible is upheld, but the Bible is always accompanied and surmounted by the wider, deeper, living tradition of the church, which is the present-day form of the Word. Among other things, this means that the Bible is not sufficient in itself to give access to the Word and is not the final norm for faith and practice. The Bible needs to be supplemented by the *Catechism of the Catholic Church*, which is 'a significant expression of the living Tradition of the Church and a sure norm for teaching the faith' (74).[3]

Thus, *VD* maintains a dynamic view of the Word whereby the Bible is a divinely appointed container of the Word. Yet the final reference point of the Word is the church from which the Bible comes and through which the present-day Word of God resounds.

Never Scripture alone

Lots of questions arise from the picture painted by *VD*, which is totally coherent with Vatican II and indeed the Council of Trent. Since *VD* is not a systematic treatise but rather a written exhortation, only a few points are dealt with in terms of explaining how the church relates to the Word.

1 The role of 'private revelations' (e.g. Marian visions and continuing revelations accredited by the Roman Catholic Church). Besides the Bible, private revelations 'introduce new emphases, [and] give rise to new forms of piety, or deepen older ones' (14). They are the basis for the Marian cults of Lourdes, Fatima and Medjugorje, for example. For evangelicals, these cults cannot be squared with basic biblical teaching, yet the normative point for 'private revelations' is the church's tradition, not the Bible alone. For Roman Catholicism, basing the faith on the Bible is important yet inconclusive. There are further standards for spiritual discernment that go beyond Scripture.

2 The 'ecclesial' reading of the Bible. According to *VD*, Scripture must never be read on one's own. Reading must always be an 'ecclesial experience', that is, something done in communion with the church. The issue at stake is not only methodological, as if private readings

---

3   The point was even more recently reinforced in the 2011 document by the (Roman Catholic) International Theological Commission entitled *Theology Today: Perspectives, principles and criteria* where it is argued that Christianity is not a 'religion of the book' but a 'religion of the word of God'. The former is 'a written and mute word', while the latter is 'the incarnate and living Word' (n. 7). A sharp distinction is made between the written Word and the living Word as if the two could possibly be polarized. The Catholic Word contains both the Scriptures 'as an inspired testimony to revelation' and 'the Church's living Tradition' (n. 8). Scripture and Tradition constitute the 'supreme rule of faith'. The text can be found here: <Theology Today: Perspectives, Principles and Criteria (2011) (vatican.va)>.

were to be replaced by study groups at a parish level presided over by a priest, but also hermeneutical. 'An authentic interpretation of the Bible must always be in harmony with the faith of the Catholic Church' (30). According to Rome, the reading of the Bible needs to be an exercise done in accordance with the institutional church, both in its forms and outcomes. Arguably, there is much wisdom in these statements, especially considering the real risks of fancy, individualistic or awkward interpretations by isolated readers of the Bible. Yet, there is something missing here. For a church that has forbidden for centuries the reading of the Bible in vernacular languages, it is at least unfortunate that not a single word of repentance is offered. For a church that has prevented its people from having access to the Bible until fifty years ago, it is at least puzzling that not a single word is spent to underline the church's need for self-correction and vigilance.

Moreover, if reading the Bible must always be done under the rule of the institution, what happens if the institution itself is caught in error, heresy or apostasy? How does the Spirit correct a sinful church if not by the biblical Word? In the history of the church, the teaching of the Bible had sometimes to be played *against* the institutional church and *against* its consensus. Only a self-proclaimed indefectible church can require total submission to 'the watchful eye of the sacred magisterium' (45) without having a final, ultimate bar. Here at stake is the question: who has the final word? The Bible or the Roman Catholic Church? Since the church is 'the home of the word' (52), *VD* responds: the latter!

3 The liturgical context of a proper approach to Scripture. Reading the Bible as an ecclesial experience means that it needs to occur in a liturgical context set forth by the Roman Catholic Church:

> The privileged place for the prayerful reading of sacred Scripture is the liturgy, and particularly the Eucharist, in which, as we celebrate the Body and Blood of Christ in the sacrament, the word itself is present and at work in our midst.
> (*VD* 86)

The hearing of God's Word is fruitful when certain conditions are present: the administration of the Eucharist (54) and other sacraments (61), the Liturgy of the Hours (62), the practice of gaining indulgences (87) and recital of the Holy Rosary (88). According to *VD*, the Bible can never be *alone* but must always be surrounded by ecclesiastical paraphernalia which inform, direct and govern biblical reading and interpretation. In so doing, the Bible is never *free* to guide the church but always conditioned by some extrabiblical practices of the church.

After centuries of stigmatization if not prohibition of the use of Bible translations in vernacular languages, the Bible is finally accessible to the Roman Catholic people. Official documents are replete with Bible quotations. Pope Francis gives a short daily homily based on Scripture, focusing on a kind of sacramental–existential reading of it but often missing the redemptive flow of the Bible. There are some lay movements which encourage a spirituality that gives Scripture a significant role. The theological framework of Vatican II, though, while recognizing the importance of Scripture in the life of the church, has placed it within the context of Tradition (with a capital 'T'), which precedes and exceeds the Bible, and which ultimately speaks through the magisterium of the church.

'Revelation', 'the Bible', 'the Word of God' – all are terms shared by Catholics and evangelicals. However, though pronounced in the same way and carrying some overlapping meaning, they come from and lead to worlds apart.

The cross, the church and the Eucharist

The cross of Jesus Christ lies at the centre of the Christian message. Jesus and 'him crucified' (e.g. 1 Cor. 2:2) summarizes the work of salvation that the Son of God has wrought for us, including his sufferings and death. The gospel has a cruciform shape in that the cross is the gateway to understanding atonement for sin, forgiveness of sins, the triumph over evil and the manifestation of the character of God. The once-and-for-all accomplishment of the death of Christ (Heb. 9:26) is the assurance that what was needed was paid for and our salvation does not need any further addition. Living under the cross is also the pattern of the Christian life.[4]

The *Catechism of the Catholic Church* affirms the uniqueness (614, 618) and perfection (529) of Christ's sacrifice on the cross of Calvary. The uniqueness of salvation history intersects, however, with the eucharistic developments in such a way that what is affirmed about the sacrifice of Christ becomes integrated with the language of re-presentation (1366), perpetuation (611, 1323) and making present (1362). The cross is appropriated through the sacrament of the Eucharist. The Eucharist is the sacrifice of Christ re-enacted, perpetuated and made present. Among other things, this means that as the cross is a sacrifice, so too the Eucharist is a sacrifice (1330, 1365), to the point where together they are 'one single sacrifice' (1367). The uniqueness of the cross is explained in loose terms in order to include the Eucharist. The work of the cross, therefore, is considered definitive but not final. Above all, it is unable to actualize its own efficacy without the active participation of the church in making it present. Given the fact that the enactment of the Eucharist is a supplement necessary in making the cross effective, it is in the Mass that the real work of redemption is carried out (1364).[5]

Even a quick perusal of the content of the *Catechism* will show a striking contrast between a just sketched theology of the cross and a fully developed sacramentology: a sober presentation of the atonement of Christ, on the one hand, and a majestic depiction of the sacrament of the Eucharist, on the other. Even from a quantitative point of view, there is an outstanding disproportion in the economy of the whole *Catechism* between the brief way in which Christ's death is treated (fewer than thirty paragraphs) and the detailed exposition of the sacrament of the Eucharist which covers almost a hundred paragraphs (1322–1419). Theologically, this quantitative

---

4 See the classic works by L. Morris, *The Cross in the New Testament* (Grand Rapids, MI: Eerdmans, 1965; repr. 1999); D. M. Lloyd-Jones, *The Cross: God's way of salvation* (Eastbourne: Kingsway, 1986); J. Stott, *The Cross of Christ* (Leicester: Inter-Varsity Press, 1986).

5 For a more detailed analysis see my article 'The cross and the Eucharist: the doctrine of the atonement according to the Catechism of the Catholic Church', *European Journal of Theology* 8.1 (1999), pp. 49–59.

disproportion involves an entire shift of attributed importance from the redemptive significance of Christ's sacrifice on Calvary to the eucharistic re-presentation of that sacrifice.

We are confronted here with a crucial point: the *Catechism* is far more interested in presenting the eucharistic re-presentation and the sacramental actualization of the atonement than its once-and-for-all historical occurrence and salvific achievement. Of course, Roman Catholicism does not perceive the distinction between the cross-offering and the Mass-offering as a polarization or contraposition between two conflicting elements, as if one would imply the exclusion of the other and vice versa. The catholic mindset is able to conjugate the two offerings in such a way as to overcome their reciprocal exclusiveness. Having said that, the standing impression is that the 'whenever' of the Eucharist supersedes the 'once only' of Calvary, the altar absorbs the cross and the sacramental system encapsulates the redemptive event. In the light of this sustained emphasis, it is not at all surprising to read the *Catechism* stating in a rather doxological vein that 'the Eucharist is the source and summit of the Christian life' (1324, which is actually a quotation from *LG* 11) or again that it is 'the sum and summary of our faith' (1327). No parallel statements, or at least comparable ones, are applied to the cross, and this difference is stark for those of an evangelical sensitivity.

We will not dwell here on studying the *Catechism* on *why, how, when, where* and *by whom* the Eucharist is celebrated. Rather, we are concerned with *what* is celebrated in the Eucharist in terms of the nexus between the once-and-for-all event of Calvary and the continuing celebration of the Eucharist.

First of all, it is important to pinpoint the language employed by the *Catechism* to refer to the Eucharist with regard to the cross. Having in view a sort of basic definition, it is argued that the Eucharist 're-presents (makes present) the sacrifice of the cross, because it is its memorial and because it applies its fruit' (1366). Other expressions include the following: the Eucharist 'perpetuates the sacrifice of the cross throughout the ages' (1323); it is the perpetuation of Jesus' offering (611); it 'makes present the one sacrifice of Christ the Saviour' (1330); it 'is the memorial of Christ's Passover, the making present and the sacramental offering of his unique sacrifice' (1362); in it 'the sacrifice of Christ offered once for all on the cross remains ever present' (1364). Widening the scope of the magisterial teaching to earlier documents, the eucharistic vocabulary becomes even richer. In the encyclical *Mediator Dei* (1947), for instance, Pope Pius XII wrote that the Eucharist 'represents', 're-enacts', 'symbolizes' (*figurant*), 'renews' (*perpetuo in Ecclesia renovari iubet*) and 'shows forth' (*mirando quodam modo ostenditur*) the sacrifice of the cross.[6] Apart from the complex terminology adopted, here again the *Catechism* does not pursue further the delineation of the theological connotation of such words.

What is altogether clear is that, in the catholic understanding of the connection between Calvary and the Eucharist, the cross-offering is inextricably related to the Mass-offering. The latter has to be understood as a renewal and perpetuation of the former but essentially linked with it. The Eucharist is regarded not as a complement to or a reduplication of the cross, but as its sacramental re-enactment within the liturgical gathering of the church. In this respect, it has to be pointed out that the popular evangelical critique of Roman eucharistic teaching is wrong when it attributes to Roman Catholicism the view that the Eucharist is a *repetition* of the cross. It is not a repetition, but something subtly different!

So interwoven is the Eucharist with the cross in Roman Catholic teaching that the two sacrifices are considered as 'one single sacrifice' (1367), though as we have already seen, the cross is also said to be a 'unique' sacrifice. Apparently, the *tetelestai* of John 19:30 ('It is finished') and the *hapax* ('once-and-for-all') theme of the letter to the Hebrews and Jude are understood dynamically as to include subsequent enactments of the same sacrifice. The Roman Catholic concept of time allows such an elastic interpretation.

Coming back to the relationship between the cross and the Eucharist, the victim of the sacrifice is the same, whereas the manner is different: bloody as for the former, unbloody as for the latter (1367). The unbloody sacrifice of the Eucharist is the bloody sacrifice of

---

6   Denz. 3840–3855.

Calvary made present in the mysterious presence of Christ in the consecrated host, in virtue of the heavenly priestly ministry of Jesus, and as a pledge of the church's union with him as his body. To show the continuity of the Catholic Church's teaching in this respect, the *Catechism* quotes the Council of Trent ('the bloody sacrifice which he [Christ] was to accomplish once for all on the cross would be re-presented, its memory perpetuated until the end of the world, and its salutary power be applied to the forgiveness of the sins we daily commit' [1366])[7] and other various Vatican II documents.[8] It is apparent throughout that the axis of Trent–Vatican II forms the strong backbone of the *Catechism* on the Eucharist.

Because it is a single sacrifice with the cross, the Eucharist has also redemptive value and effects. In fact, the *Catechism* maintains that 'as often as the sacrifice of the Cross by which "Christ our Pasch has been sacrificed" is celebrated on the altar, the work of redemption is carried out' (1364, quoting *LG* 3). The Council of Trent spoke of the Eucharist as being also 'truly propitiatory';[9] in the *Catechism*, this propitiatory connotation of the Eucharist has dropped out in the sense that it is not repeated explicitly. However, the Tridentine theology of eucharistic propitiation remains basically unaltered in that the Eucharist has both a sacrificial status and a redemptive function.

So far, we have seen that the *Catechism* has focused on the historical event of the atonement and, with a much more detailed theological construction, on the sacramental events which re-enact it. The link between the cross-offering and the eucharistic offering is one of the major tenets of the whole Roman Catholic under-standing of the nature of the atonement and the way in which its redemptive achievements apply to humankind. However, there is yet another key element of extraordinary dogmatic weight which stems from the teaching of the *Catechism* and which belongs to the core of the Roman Catholic faith.

---

7   Other references to Trent are in §§ 1337, 1367, 1371, 1374, 1376, 1377, 1394.
8   §§ 1323, 1324, 1344, 1346, 1364, 1369, 1373, 1388, 1392, 1399, 1405.
9   Denz. 1743, 1753.

At the end of the section on the passion and death of Jesus Christ, the *Catechism* makes reference to 'our participation in Christ's sacrifice' (618), where 'our' stands for the collective participation of all who, by means of the incarnation, are somehow united with Christ (cf. *GS* 22,2). It has to be said that, for Roman Catholicism, 'our participation' has a distinct ecclesial significance, meaning the church's participation. This clause – 'our participation in Christ's sacrifice' – should immediately sound an alarm bell in Protestant ears inasmuch as the uniqueness, sufficiency, completeness and finality of the cross cannot contemplate any sort of addition, supplementation or contribution on our part as church. If it is Christ's, it is not ours, in the sense that we do not actively participate in it but only thankfully and undeservedly receive its gracious benefits by faith. Of course, the church's actual taking part in the sacrifice of Christ is instead perfectly legitimate, indeed a sheer truism, within the Roman Catholic dogmatic framework. Where a Protestant sensitivity perceives an incompatibility, indeed an impossibility of any form of synergism between the perfect work of Christ and our response to it, the Roman Catholic mindset allows, indeed requires, that what is attributable to Christ somehow pertains to the church as well. According to the *Catechism*, which at this point quotes *Gaudium et Spes* 22,5, the possibility of being partners in the paschal mystery is offered to everybody (618). This rather cryptic expression is not spelt out at this point but just inserted prolectically, so as to anticipate what will follow in a subsequent stage.

In order to receive clarifications on the matter, we have to refer to the section on the ecclesial aspects of the Eucharist, where the teaching on the way in which this participation in Christ's sacrifice has to be apprehended is unfolded. The *Catechism* envisages an ecclesial active participation in the sacramental enactment of the Eucharist. Not only is the Eucharist the sacramental re-presentation of Christ's sacrifice but it is also the sacramental enactment of the sacrifice of the church. The church's involvement is so prominent that the Eucharist itself is said to be the 'memorial of the sacrifice of Christ and his body, the church' (1362). In the Eucharist, 'the sacrifice of Christ becomes also the sacrifice of the members of the body'

(1368) and therefore it 'includes the Church's offering' (1330). In the sacramental act, the church is the recipient of the benefits of the Eucharist, but it is also the active agent, the offering party, and because it is the body of Christ, the church itself is the content of the offering. The Eucharist is something offered *for* the church but also *from* the church and *by* the church (1118). The church is so directly involved in what happens in the Eucharist that what is offered in the Eucharist is *its* offering, *its* sacrifice. It is also true that, according to the *Catechism*, the church's sacrifice is never isolated from its Head, as if it were *another* sacrifice, but, on the contrary, the church offers it *in* Christ, *with* Christ and *through* Christ (1368), thus being the one and the same sacrifice of Christ (1367).

Here, the Roman Catholic understanding of the *unio mystica* (mystical union) between Christ and the church is fully in view and forms the theological background against which the whole discourse of the *Catechism* on the participation of the church in the sacrifice of Christ needs to be located. In the Eucharist, Christ and the church are so closely intertwined that, as Irish Jesuit theologian Raymond Moloney has maintained, 'the one who offers is the one who is offered, namely the body of Christ, Head and members, now united in one great communion of worship'.[10] In the Eucharist, the relationship between Christ and church is thought of as belonging to the categories of head and members, forming together the whole Christ, the *totus Christus* (795). Head and members are united in the offering of the Eucharist.

So, the mode of participation of the church in the sacrifice of Christ is sacramental; the event in which the participation takes place is the Eucharist; the theological rationale which warrants participation is the mystical union between Christ and the church, head and members, who form one body (1119, 793); the content of the sacrifice includes the church itself in that the church, as the members of the mystical body, cannot be separated from the Head which is offered. Inseparably connected to these crucial elements of the doctrine of the Eucharist is the centrality and agency of the

---

10 R. Moloney, 'The doctrine of the Eucharist', in M. J. Walsh (ed.), *Commentary on the Catechism of the Catholic Church* (London: Geoffrey Chapman, 1994), p. 267.

church. If the Eucharist is the re-presentation of the sacrifice of Christ, then the subject (the church) that offers the sacrifice assumes a decisive role in the workings of it. That is, it not only receives its benefits but also actualizes them and carries out its memorial. The theology of re-presentation can be explained in terms of the violation of the uniqueness and soteriological completeness of the sacrifice of Christ by an enlarged view of the sacrifice which includes both the unique event of the cross and the continual events of the Mass. The Roman Catholic theology of the Eucharist, 'the fount and apex of the whole Christian life' (*LG* 11), is a consequence of a prior intrusion of 'church time' into the time of Christ, which in turn establishes a continuity between them in terms of the extension of the incarnation of the Son within the mission of the church.

In the end, the sacramental and ecclesial attachments to the work of Christ, which we have clearly seen in the *Catechism*, deprive the atoning death of Christ of its finality because, though it is considered as paramount, the cross is not appreciated as efficacious per se. By ascribing to the Eucharist the possibility of applying the fruits of the cross to human beings, the *Catechism* makes the response of faith necessary but not sufficient in order to be saved. Moreover, by assigning to the church a highly Christological status with quasi-ontological overtones, the *Catechism* makes room for the church to play a cooperative role in salvation. Therefore, the difference on these matters is still with us, as wide and fundamental as ever.

Salvation, justification and regeneration

The evangelical understanding of the gospel stands on two pillars: the authority of Scripture as God's Word written (the formal principle) and justification by grace alone through faith alone (the material principle). Scripture is the norm for the Christian life; justification is the ground of it. On the basis of biblical texts such as Romans 3:23–26; 4:5–8 and 5:18–19, J. I. Packer lucidly condenses the scriptural teaching on justification as follows:

> [Justification is] God's act of remitting the sins of, and reckon-
> ing righteousness to, ungodly sinners freely, by his grace,
> through faith in Christ, on the ground not of their own works,
> but of the representative righteousness and substitutionary
> blood-shedding of Jesus Christ on their behalf.[11]

This is the heart of Christianity. Historically, justification has been the landmark of the biblical faith since the times of the apostles. The Protestant Reformation of the sixteenth century reinforced its centrality and corrected many mistakes of the medieval church.

From Trent to the *Joint Declaration on the Doctrine of Justification* (*JDDJ*)

The Roman Catholic Church at the time of the Reformation reacted negatively to the Reformers' account of justification and came out with an alternative view. At the Council of Trent (1545–63) Rome continued to use the word 'justification' but filled it with a completely different meaning. For Trent justification was a process rather than an act of God; a process initiated by the sacrament of baptism where the righteousness of God was thought to be infused; a process nurtured by the religious works of the faithful and sustained by the sacramental system of the church; a process needing to include a time of purification in purgatory, before perhaps being enacted on judgment day. Rome reframed justification in terms of a combination of God's initiative and the efforts of human beings. Grace and works joined together, resulting in a continuing journey of justification, ultimately dependent on human works and sacraments. This confused and confusing teaching has been misleading people ever since.

The most recent Roman Catholic statement on justification is the 1999 *Joint Declaration on the Doctrine of Justification* signed between Rome and the World Lutheran Federation.[12] The word 'justification'

---

11 J. I. Packer, *God's Words: Studies in key biblical themes* (Grand Rapids, MI: Baker, 1988), p. 139.
12 For a more detailed analysis of Trent and *JDDJ*, see my chapter 'Not by faith alone? An analysis of the Roman Catholic doctrine of justification from Trent to the Joint Declaration', in M. Barrett (ed.), *The Doctrine on Which the Church Stands or Falls: Justification in biblical, theological, historical, and pastoral perspective* (Wheaton, IL: Crossway, 2019), pp. 739–767.

lies at the centre of the document, but it has a different meaning from the biblical one. It presents a non-tragic view of sin; the necessity of the sacramental system of the church; and an emphasis on the universalist scope of justification. The blurred distinction between justification and the response to it are all factors that make the meaning of the word different from the biblical meaning. *JDDJ* gives voice to the present-day common understanding of justification shared by both the Roman Catholic Church and the liberal churches. What is missing both at Trent and in *JDDJ* is the declarative, forensic act of justification, the exclusive grounding in divine grace, the full assurance of being justified because of what God the Father has declared, God the Son has achieved and God the Spirit has worked out.

Grace alone?

Many commentators with good intentions, even on the evangelical side, have rightly given attention to what seems to be the heart of the 1999 *JDDJ*. Paragraph 15 solemnly says:

> By grace alone, in faith in Christ's saving work and not because of any merit on our part, we are accepted by God and receive the Holy Spirit, who renews our hearts while equipping and calling us to good works.

If read out of context and in a theologically naive way, this sentence could be a relevant and pointed summary of the biblical message concerning the mode of justification (by grace only and not based on merits), the means of justification (by faith alone), the grounds of justification (the saving work of Christ) and the consequences of justification (divine adoption and the gift of the Holy Spirit, the renewal of the heart and the activation of the Christian life). However, every sound exercise in theological hermeneutics, including the reading of the documents of any ecumenical dialogue, must take into account the immediate and more general context, the meaning of the words used and the consequences of what is being claimed. Taken out of context, No. 15 would make much sense from an evangelical perspective.[13] Yet it must be considered as an integral part of *JDDJ* and therefore must be understood in relation to the whole document.

Sacramental grace

When approaching the various aspects of the doctrine of justification, the Catholic and Lutheran churches agree on a sacramental understanding of grace. It is this sacramental framework that qualifies the reference to the expression 'by grace alone' contained in No. 15. Together, in fact, they declare that 'by the action of the Holy Spirit in baptism, they [the sinners] are granted the gift of salvation' (25), thus undermining the idea that it is only by grace that God saves sinners through faith alone. Lutheran theology, with its doctrine of regenerational baptism, actually runs this risk. Later, in No. 28, *JDDJ* states (always with both parties affirming this together) that 'in baptism the Holy Spirit unites one with Christ, justifies, and truly renews the person'. It is not surprising, however, that the Catholic clarification on this point forcefully underlines that 'persons are justified through baptism as hearers of the word and believers in it' (27). On the one hand, then, *JDDJ* wants to affirm the importance of the declaration of the righteousness of God received by faith. On the other, though, it reiterates the need for sacramental action through the mediation of the church as essential for justification and, therefore, for salvation.

The Roman Catholic point is further reinforced through the claim, accepted by Catholics, that the grace of Jesus Christ is 'imparted' in baptism (30). According to this view, grace is not received by faith alone but is granted by God through the church, which administers it in baptism. This statement cannot be reconciled with the view according to which salvation is by grace alone apart from works, even sacramental ones. So, for all the good intentions expressed by the producers of this document and the admirable effort made in dialogue, the result is below expectations and beyond an obedient adherence to the biblical Word of God. In contemporary Roman Catholicism

---

13 References to *JDDJ* will be indicated by numbered paragraphs in the main body of the text.

we see a total consistency with respect to the traditional doctrine, that is, that justification occurs at baptism by a sacramental act.

For the Catholic Church, the phrase 'by grace alone' of No. 15 in *JDDJ* means that grace is intrinsically, constitutionally and necessarily linked to the sacrament, and thus to the church that administers it and the works implemented by it. In this view, salvation cannot be by grace alone, unless 'grace alone' is understood as the same grace being organically incorporated into the sacrament of the church. We are evidently in the presence of a different concept of grace. In *JDDJ* there is an attempt to redescribe this theological understanding of salvation in language that looks like the Lutheran style (which the Catholic Church appropriates through the use of such expressions as 'by grace alone' of No. 15 and the recognition that works 'follow justification and are its fruits' of No. 37). However, this new description does not give the impression of change in the theology of the Council of Trent (1545–63), according to which grace is sacramental and seen within a synergistic dynamic of the process of salvation. This understanding of grace appears to be more in line with the Catholic heritage of the Council of Trent, in an updated form, than with classic Protestant theology. In this sense, *JDDJ* is a clear exercise in an increased 'catholicity' (i.e. the ability to absorb ideas without changing the core) on the part of Rome, which has not become more evangelical in the biblical sense.

Roman Catholicism sees justification as a gradual and progressive process through which the righteousness of Christ is increasingly infused into a person and is therefore not seen as a declarative act of God through which the righteousness of Christ is imputed to the sinner. Justification is not a theological relic of a distant past. It is indeed key for grasping the good news of Christ. Roman Catholicism uses the same word but has a completely different understanding and explanation of the theology of that word, massively affecting its practice.

From justification to regeneration

The doctrine of regeneration belongs to the core of the biblical view of salvation, and 'regeneration' is a term that is shared by all Christian traditions in their respective accounts of what it means to be saved.[14] To be regenerated by God is the act by which God himself re-creates life in an otherwise dead person. Regeneration is, therefore, the entry point of a saved life. Surveying the biblical evidence (e.g. 2 Cor. 5:17; Gal. 6:15), Packer summarizes it in this way: regeneration 'means rebirth (*palingenesia*): it speaks of a creative renovation wrought by the power of God'.[15] On the surface, the theological meaning of the word is quite clear and all Christian traditions acknowledge it. The difference between them is not so much in the word itself as in the theological 'worlds' in which they implant the word in order to make sense of it.

The *Catechism* uses the term 'regeneration' by associating it with other biblical and liturgical words and expressions that contribute towards its definition. In doing so, it approximately indicates the meaning of regeneration by way of connecting it to similar words. As a life-giving event, regeneration is related to 'new birth' or 'rebirth' (e.g. 1213, 1270). Therefore, the *Catechism* translates the Greek-derived word ('regeneration') into the birth-related words. In another metaphorical area, regeneration is linked to the transition from darkness to light (e.g. 1250) and to the inner renewal of one's own self and purification from sin (e.g. 1262). Moreover, regeneration is further associated with entering the kingdom of God (1263). There are occasional biblical references to support each meaning.

What is most striking, however, is the relationship that the *Catechism* envisages between regeneration and the sacrament of baptism. More than its biblical nuances and theological significance, it is this inherent association that ultimately defines the Roman Catholic understanding of the core of regeneration.

Sacramental regeneration

As is well known, the *Catechism* is structured according to the order of the Apostles' Creed (the profession of faith), followed by the presentation of the sacraments (the celebration of the Christian mystery),

---

14 Here I reuse materials already published in the article 'Same word, different worlds: the Roman Catholic doctrine of regeneration', *Credo* (July 2013), pp. 64–71.
15 Packer, *God's Words*, p. 149.

the Christian life, including the Ten Commandments (life in Christ), and the life of prayer, which is centred on the Lord's Prayer. In this overall framework, it is interesting to notice where regeneration is theologically placed and treated. It is not found in the section on the work of Christ, nor in the section on the ministry of the Holy Spirit, but instead comes to the fore in the second part which deals with the sacraments of the church. Doctrinally, then, regeneration, though organically related to the work of the triune God, is specifically attached to the sacramental ministry of the church. From a systematic point of view, the Roman Catholic theological map places regeneration under the rubric of the liturgy of the church rather than in the chapter on God's salvation.

More specifically, it is the sacrament of baptism that plays a fundamental role in bringing regeneration about. It is in the context of baptism that the Catholic doctrine of regeneration is spelt out:

> Holy Baptism is the basis of the whole Christian life, the gateway to life in the Spirit (*vitae spiritualis ianua*), and the door which gives access to the other sacraments. Through Baptism we are freed from sin and reborn as sons of God; we become members of Christ, are incorporated into the Church and made sharers in her mission: 'Baptism is the sacrament of regeneration through water in the word.'
> (*CCC* 1213)

The final quote in the above passage comes from the 1566 *Roman Catechism* (II, 2, 5), which was published as a result of the Council of Trent. Notice, however, that no scriptural reference is given to support the doctrine, but rather it appears as the combination of different biblical words which are given a sacramental bent. Such an absence of biblical support is telling. Indeed, there is no biblical evidence to support such a weighty doctrinal statement. In the *Catechism*, baptism is seen as the sacrament which accords to human beings freedom from sin and rebirth as children of God. As regeneration is the result of baptism and baptism is administered by the church, it is syllogistically evident that regeneration does not happen as an act of

God's grace alone, to be received by faith alone, but as an act mediated by the sacrament of the church, which enacts its intended result.

Expanding its teaching on baptism as that which effects regeneration, the *Catechism* goes on to say that, 'This sacrament is also called "the washing of regeneration and renewal by the Holy Spirit," for it signifies and actually brings about the birth of water and the Spirit' (1215). This time the language comes directly from Titus 3:5 but fails to indicate that the biblical passage puts the 'washing of regeneration' in the context of God's goodness and loving-kindness, stressing that we are not saved because of 'works done by us' but out of 'his own mercy'. The focus of the whole passage is God alone working out his loving plan of salvation without any contribution on the part of human beings or the church – any work of any kind. In the *Catechism*, however, it is the sacrament that 'signifies and actually brings about' regeneration. It is the act of baptism that causes the new birth to occur *ex opere operato* (from the work done). The emphasis has shifted from the merciful God who regenerates a person out of his sovereign grace to the baptizing church that performs the sacrament of regeneration. In other words, a major shift has taken place: from the graceful act of divine salvation to the participation of the church in the saving act, and from the free gift of God to the ecclesiastical sacrament administered by the priest.

According to the *Catechism*, the time of regeneration is when baptism is administered. It is the baptized person who is regenerated and therefore enters the sacramental life of the church in whose sacraments he or she will receive the fullness of salvation. It is through baptism that the person is forgiven for all his or her sins (1263), made a new creature, adopted as a child of God, and becomes a member of Christ, a co-heir with him and a temple of the Holy Spirit (1265). It is in baptism that the person receives 'sanctifying grace, the grace of justification' (1266),[16] and is incorporated into the

---

16 These terms here are confusing for a Protestant reader: 'sanctifying grace' is defined as 'the grace of justification', therefore significantly blurring sanctification and justification. Ecumenical advocates tell us that the 1999 official Roman Catholic–Lutheran *Joint Declaration on the Doctrine of Justification* reached a substantial agreement on *sola fide*. The reality is that the *Catechism* (which is far more authoritative than the just mentioned text) keeps on confusing sanctification and justification, as the Council of Trent did in the sixteenth century.

church (1267–1270). It is baptism that is the sacramental bond of the unity of Christians (1271), therefore warranting the Roman Catholic view that Christian unity is based on baptism.

The 'sacramental economy'

The above view of baptismal regeneration is part of the Roman Catholic view of the sacraments. The *Catechism* defines this theological framework as the 'sacramental economy' of the Christian faith (1076). If we read what the *Catechism* says about regeneration without grasping what the 'sacramental economy' means, we will completely misread it. To put it succinctly, the 'sacramental economy' is a view that binds God to act through the sacraments and therefore through the church.[17] Everything that God does, he does through the sacraments. His grace comes to us through the sacraments. His salvation reaches us through the sacraments. His work has an impact on us through the sacraments. The problem is not the recognition of the biblical importance of the sacraments but their exclusivity in terms of what God can do. In the background of the sacraments, there is always the church that administers them, having therefore a fundamental role in mediating God's actions. The word 'regeneration' means new birth received from God, but the world of the 'sacramental economy' makes it a church affair because God is believed to bind himself to work only through the sacraments of the church. His grace is always mediated through the church.

This point is crucial even beyond the specific topic under consideration. When evangelicals deal with Roman Catholic theology, they tend to overlook the 'sacramental dimension' of the Roman Church. They analyse common words, common concerns and common language in an atomistic way and may come to the conclusion that the old divisions are over because the language is similar. But this cannot be true because the Roman Catholic system makes them signify something different from, and even opposed to, the plain gospel meaning.

---

17 In a more technical way, the *Catechism* speaks of the 'sacramental economy' as 'the communication of the fruits of Christ's Paschal mystery in the celebration of the Church's sacramental liturgy' (1076).

Mission and unity

'Mission' is another word that stands at the intersection of many Christian accounts of our faith. From Roman Catholics to ecumenical Protestants, many place 'mission' at the centre of their vision and agenda. It is therefore important to go beyond common phonetics and to explore whether or not there is a common theology of mission. The Second Vatican Council placed great emphasis on 'mission', and one of its documents (i.e. the decree *Ad Gentes*) is entirely dedicated to presenting the missionary vision of the Roman Catholic Church in the modern world. In 1990 Pope John Paul II issued *Redemptoris Missio*, an encyclical on the permanent validity of the missionary mandate of the church that encouraged its continuing missionary activity. It is clear that Catholic missiology is active, and 'mission' is a key descriptor of what Roman Catholicism stands for and seeks to do.

The joy of the gospel?

The highly acclaimed apostolic exhortation *Evangelii Gaudium* (The Joy of the Gospel, 2013) is considered to be the manifesto for Pope Francis's view of the Christian faith and the mission of the Roman Catholic Church.[18] He writes, 'Throughout the world, let us be permanently in a state of mission' (25). These programmatic words epitomize his missionary vision. Without a doubt, mission is central to his thought and action and is a defining mark of his pontificate. Having said that, it is not always clear what he means when he talks about 'mission'. Indeed, in today's religious language 'mission' is one of those words which can have multiple 'shades of grey', and discovering its meaning can become a conundrum. Pope Francis adds his own complexities and nuances to the already variegated semantic range of the word 'mission'.

In *The Joy of the Gospel*, the 'heart' of the gospel is summarized in this way: it is 'the beauty of the saving love of God made manifest in Jesus Christ who died and rose from the dead' (36). On the surface

18 <www.vatican.va/content/francesco/en/apost_exhortations/documents/papa-francesco_esortazione-ap_20131124_evangelii-gaudium.html>

this appears to be an impeccable condensation of the core of the gospel message. Yet, after reading it carefully, one needs to come to terms with some blind spots. In this apparently evangelical definition of the gospel something is missing: while the objective good news of God is rightly related to the narrative of Jesus Christ, the subjective part of it (i.e. repentance from one's own sin and personal faith) is omitted.

The tragedy of being lost without Jesus Christ is also downplayed because nowhere in the document are unbelievers called on to repent and believe in Jesus Christ. On the contrary, all people are affirmed as they already are and where they already stand. In the papal document, non-Catholic Christians are already united in baptism (244), Jews don't need to convert (247), and with believing Muslims the way is 'dialogue' because 'together with us they adore the one, merciful God' (252, a quotation of *LG* 16).[19] Other non-Christians are also 'justified by the grace of God' and are associated with 'the paschal mystery of Jesus Christ' (254). The gospel appears not to be a message of salvation from God's judgment but instead one of access to a fuller measure of a salvation that is already given to all humankind. According to Francis, therefore, mission is the joyful willingness to extend the fullness of grace to a world that is already under grace.

In a nutshell, what the pope writes *is* the problem of Roman Catholicism. On the one hand, it uses standard and common Christian vocabulary. On the other, it uses it and interprets it in such a way as to depart from essential components of the biblical gospel.

Mission without apologetics?

Is this critical assessment based on reading too much into the pope's gospel omissions? One way of answering this question is to allow the pope to speak for himself in explaining his missionary vision. Luckily, while flying back from Myanmar and Bangladesh (3 December 2017), Francis gave a telling comment on how he sees mission as it relates to apologetics. Here is the script of the in-flight

---

19 On this issue, see the insightful book by A. Bannister, *Do Muslims and Christians Worship the Same God?* (London: IVP, 2021).

conference, during which Francis replied to a question posed by a journalist representing KTO (French Catholic Television).[20] The question-and-answer session is worth quoting at length:

Etienne Loraillere (KTO): Holiness, there is a question from the group of journalists from France. Some are opposed to inter-religious dialogue and evangelization. During this trip you have spoken of dialogue for building peace. But, what is the priority? Evangelizing or dialoguing for peace? Because to evangelize means bringing about conversions that provoke tension and sometimes provoke conflicts between believers. So, what is the priority, evangelizing or dialoguing? Thanks.

Pope Francis: First distinction: evangelizing is not making proselytism. The Church grows not for proselytism but for attraction, that is for testimony, this was said by Pope Benedict XVI. What is evangelization like? Living the Gospel and bearing witness to how one lives the Gospel, witnessing to the Beatitudes, giving testimony to Matthew 25, the Good Samaritan, forgiving 70 times 7 and in this witness the Holy Spirit works and there are conversions, but we are not very enthusiastic to make conversions immediately. If they come, they wait, you speak, your tradition . . . seeking that a conversion be the answer to something that the Holy Spirit has moved in my heart before the witness of the Christians.

During the lunch I had with the young people at World Youth Day in Krakow, 15 or so young people from the entire world, one of them asked me this question: what do I have to say to a classmate at the university, a friend, good, but he is atheist . . . what do I have to say to change him, to convert him? The answer was this: the last thing you have to do is say something. You live your Gospel and if he asks you why you do this, you can explain why you do it. And let the Holy Spirit activate him. This is the strength and the meekness of the Holy Spirit in

---

20 <www.ncregister.com/daily-news/full-text-of-pope-francis-in-flight-press-conference-from-bangladesh>.

the conversion. It is not a mental convincing, with apologetics, with reasons, it is the Spirit that makes the vocation. We are witnesses, witnesses of the Gospel. 'Testimony' is a Greek word that means martyr. Every day martyrdom, martyrdom also of blood, when it arrives. And your question: What is the priority, peace or conversion? But when you live with testimony and respect, you make peace. Peace starts to break down in this field when proselytism begins and there are so many ways of proselytism and this is not the Gospel. I don't know if I answered.

With this answer one is projected into the reality of the missiological vision of Pope Francis. Let's briefly mention its main points. First, there is a negative reference to proselytism without defining it. As it stands, his words discourage the expectation for conversions and put a stigma on the missionary activity that looks forward to seeing people embracing Christ out of their religious or secular background (see instead Mark 1:15; Acts 2:37–38). Second, there is an unnecessary polarization between good deeds/attitudes and the verbal proclamation of the gospel. Nowhere in the Bible is such a polarization maintained between the behaviour of the messenger and the content of the message. We are instead called always to join up what we say, what we do and how we do it (e.g. 1 Pet. 3:15–17). Third, there is a distrust of apologetics in dealing with unbelief. The young missionary is not expected to give reasons for what he or she believes or to challenge the belief system of the atheist friend. In this way, the pope seems to discourage engaging in meaningful apologetics (evidently against 1 Pet. 3:15).

According to Pope Francis, then, mission does not look forward to making disciples, refrains from verbally proclaiming the good news and is sceptical about apologetics. In the evangelical understanding of mission, almost everything the pope warns against is instead strongly affirmed: the verbal proclamation of the gospel of Jesus Christ and the necessity of Christian persuasion in the context of lives marked by integrity. This is not what Pope Francis has in mind when he refers to mission. The reason for this, again, is that the Roman Catholic understanding of the 'salvation' that is the end of mission is different from a biblical understanding of the same word.

A gradualist view of salvation

A test-case of the wrong turn taken by the Roman Catholic Church in its concept and practice of mission is its view of salvation as having a universal scope and a hopeful end for all. According to post-Vatican II Roman Catholicism, there are circles of salvation which ultimately embrace the whole of humanity. The Roman Catholic tradition used to operate according to the principle *extra ecclesiam nulla salus* (outside the church there is no salvation). According to a rigid interpretation of Cyprianus which took hold in the medieval church, belonging to the Catholic Church was the condition for salvation. It is clear that followers of other religions were excluded from the chance of being saved as a result of being outside the Roman institution. Here too the profound trans-formation that emerged from the Vatican II council should be underscored. In fact, the council documents deal with the change in status of non-Christian believers, just as non-Christian religions are seen in a new light. People who follow other religions, even if far away from Christianity, are not considered to be away from Christ. They are instead in some measure 'related' to Christ (*LG* 16) whether they wish it or not, whether they know it or not. If we take into account the fact that, again according to the council, Catholics enjoy a privileged relationship with Christ, being 'incorporated' with him (*LG* 11, 14, 31), Roman Catholicism is seen as a completion, the achievement of aspirations existing in non-Christian religions. The grace of God is already present in the nature of religions and the church. Because of its special prerogatives, the church is the place where spiritual longings can be taken to a higher level and accom-plish their true purpose. Here too the universalism of salvation is combined with the character of the church. Clearly, the catholicity of Rome transcends the rather narrow boundaries of Christianity and addresses the world of religions, proffering the Roman Catholic Church as the place where the legitimate claims of other religions find their fulfilment. Christianity, religions, culture, society, the whole world – these are the borders of the catholicity of Roman Catholicism.

This is the way Catholic author Jack Mulder summarizes it, quoting Paul VI and John Paul II and evoking standard Vatican II teaching: 'There are four concentric circles of people: first, all humanity; second, the worshipers of the one God; third, all Christians; and fourth, Catholics themselves.'[21] Salvation is seen as a gift that people receive in different degrees depending on the circle they choose to identify with or find themselves in. Roman Catholics receive God's grace in the fullest measure through the sacraments administered by the (Roman) church under the pope and the bishops who are the successors of the apostles. Other Christians receive God's grace to a lesser extent because they retain true elements of the faith but lack the fullness of it in not being in full fellowship with the Church of Rome. Religious people receive it because they have a sense of the divine, although they miss important aspects of the faith. Finally, the whole of humanity receives it because everyone is human and therefore existentially open to God's grace which works in mysterious ways. Ultimately, 'the only real way to get outside of God's grace is to expel oneself from it'.[22] The conditions for such self-expulsion are so remote and limited that practically there is hope that all will be saved. This is quite different from clear biblical teaching, which turns the picture upside down. According to Scripture we are all by nature 'children of wrath' (Eph. 2:3), all sinners (Rom. 3:23), all under God's judgment (John 3:18). It is not we who exclude ourselves from God's grace. Because of sin we are all born into this condition. Roman Catholicism turns the argument around and believes the contrary, namely that we are all born into God's grace, albeit at various levels of depth and at different degrees.

'Mission' is yet another example that illustrates the title and premise of this book. The word is the same, but the world being described is very different. In Francis's vocabulary (which embodies Vatican II teaching), mission does not mean going out in the world

---

21 J. Mulder Jr, *What Does It Mean to Be Catholic?* (Grand Rapids, MI: Eerdmans, 2015), p. 9.
22 Mulder, *What Does It Mean to Be Catholic?* p. 190.

to proclaim the gospel of salvation found only in Jesus. Rather, it means calling people to come closer to the salvation that all people already are part of by being human, though in different degrees. For Francis there is no 'in or out' sense in this understanding of mission. The whole of humankind is already 'in' a state of grace: mission is the task of calling people to engage with it more deeply, not to call them 'in'. They are already 'in'. Here again, the words are the same but their meaning is vastly different. Evangelicals have to do their homework in order to go beyond the surface of mere phonetics to grasp the profoundly different theological vision underpinning the Roman Catholic language. They may find it surprising how far Rome is from the standard evangelical understanding of the biblical gospel.

Trends in the Roman Catholic view of unity

'Unity' is one of the most used and perhaps abused words in the present-day Christian vocabulary. The problem is that while the word is the same, its meaning may differ significantly according to who is talking about it. Those who speak about unity may have the impression that they are talking about the same thing because they use the word 'unity', but the reality is that more careful attention is needed in order to avoid unpleasant pitfalls in understanding and communication.

Before Vatican II, the view of the Roman Catholic Church was that all non-Catholics were heretics, schismatics or pagans. You were either in the church or outside and against it. The council introduced a new way of looking at non-Catholic people and devoted one important document to ecumenism: *Unitatis Redintegratio*. While the Catholic Church retained its conviction of having access to the full sacramental salvation, other believers were considered as revolving around it according to their distance from or nearness to the centre. This was also the topic of John Paul II's 1995 encyclical *Ut Unum Sint* (That They May Be One). Other religions reflected different degrees of truth and blessing and were seen in a fundamentally positive way. The point is that each religion contained elements of truth that needed to be appreciated and that formed the basis for a rediscovered universal sense of family. Vatican II abandoned the clear-cut in–out approach to embrace the principle of graduality: instead of denouncing the others' errors, each religion came to be seen as having some good in it, thus needing to be seen as having some form of unity with the Roman Catholic Church.

Francis is the most ecumenical pope ever. Before his election to the papacy, Francis built relationships with evangelical leaders and attended evangelical conferences in his home country of Argentina. Since he became pope, Francis has visited an Italian Pentecostal church and apologized for how Roman Catholics have persecuted Pentecostals. He has welcomed hundreds upon hundreds of evangelical leaders to the Vatican. What is behind Francis's extraordinary openness and warmth towards evangelicals?

We find one answer in a fascinating article from the *Catholic Herald* titled, 'The pope's great evangelical gamble':[23]

> Somewhere in Pope Francis's office is a document that could alter the course of Christian history. It declares an end to hostilities between Catholics and Evangelicals and says the two traditions are now 'united in mission because we are declaring the same Gospel'. The Holy Father is thinking of signing the text in 2017, the 500th anniversary of the Reformation, alongside Evangelical leaders.

The author explains that the pope believes that 'the Reformation is already over' because the Lutheran World Federation and Vatican's *Joint Declaration on the Doctrine of Justification* had been signed in 1999. In a video recording shown at an evangelical pastors' conference in Texas, Francis said, 'Brothers and sisters, Luther's protest is over.'

The previous two popes, John Paul and Benedict, in response to the 1999 *JDDJ* statement, did not announce that the Reformation is over. Benedict, while still leading the Congregation of the Doctrine of the Faith, issued a second official Vatican statement which

---

23 <www.catholicherald.co.uk/the-popes-great-evangelical-gamble/>

explained that the joint statement was inadequate and listed a number of serious differences between the historic Lutheran position and the Roman Catholic position. In short, Benedict explained that the Council of Trent, which condemned central evangelical Protestant convictions as 'anathema' (i.e. cursed), was still in force.

But Francis is a different kind of pope. He is not a high-powered theologian confronting relativism or clarifying doctrine like Benedict, or a philosopher theologian like John Paul II whose Vatican produced the Roman Catholic *Catechism*. Francis is sincere, kind and loving. But he is a committed Roman Catholic ecumenical leader and, most importantly, he is doing evangelism in the same way Roman Catholics have evangelized throughout their history. Roman Catholics have extended their influence by absorbing movements, converting rulers and using physical force. This last method is no longer a widespread strategy of the Roman Catholic Church. In fact, as we have seen, Francis has rightly apologized for how Roman Catholics have persecuted Pentecostals, indigenous groups, Waldensians and so on.

But the Roman Catholic evangelistic methods of absorbing movements and converting rulers are both being actively used by Francis in his present public-relations campaign aimed at evangelicals. For example, Roman Catholicism did not reject the charismatic movement but absorbed it, and a new sort of Catholic was created, a 'charismatic Catholic'. The Roman Catholic method of absorption is now focused on evangelicalism, seeking to dismiss the differences and emphasize the shared beliefs. Or, as the *Catholic Herald* describes it, 'The pope's great evangelical gamble' is Francis's attempt to declare 'an end to hostilities between Catholics and Evangelicals'. Francis is seeking to establish a new sort of Catholic, an 'evangelical Catholic'.

The first step towards this broader absorption is the conversion of rulers. Over the previous two millennia the Catholic Church has historically extended its influence by means of converting the kings and queens of political power and, within a generation or two, their kingdoms. This same method is being used today to convert rulers of influence. Although a flood of Roman Catholics are becoming evangelicals, there is just a trickle of evangelical leaders (rulers of influence) converting to Roman Catholicism.[24]

The importance of this should not be underestimated. Evangelicalism is easily the fastest-growing Christian movement in the last century. According to Oxford University Press's *World Christian Encyclopedia*, the Roman Catholic Church stagnated with only 6% growth over a century, while evangelicalism grew 20 times as fast, with 122% growth as a percentage of the world's population.[25] Roman Catholic leaders are aware that millions of Roman Catholics each year are converting to evangelical churches all across the world. When Benedict was still pope, he gave a lecture in his home country of Germany and expressed confusion about how to respond to the enormous growth of the global evangelical church:

> The geography of Christianity has changed dramatically in recent times, and is in the process of changing further. Faced with a new form of Christianity, which is spreading with overpowering missionary dynamism, sometimes in frightening ways, the mainstream Christian denominations often seem at a loss . . . This worldwide phenomenon – that bishops from all over the world are constantly telling me about – poses a question to us all: what is this new form of Christianity saying to us, for better and for worse?[26]

But while Benedict seemed confused, Francis is bringing evangelicals close, saying we are the same and that the Reformation is over. Francis is not confused or 'at a loss'. He knows exactly what he is about.

The siren call of unity

In our fragmented and violent world, 'unity' is one of the catchwords that many people are attracted to. Francis is strongly advocating for

---

24 See the testimonies of conversion to Roman Catholicism collected by R. J. Snell and R. George (eds.), *Mind, Heart, and Soul: Intellectuals and the path to Rome* (Charlotte, NC: TAN Books, 2018).

25 D. Barrett (ed.), *World Christian Encyclopedia* (Oxford: Oxford University Press, 1982).

26 <www.vatican.va/content/benedict-xvi/en/speeches/2011/september/documents/hf_ben-xvi_spe_20110923_evangelical-church-erfurt.html>

Christian unity and ultimately the unity of humankind. His passion for unity makes many evangelicals think that he is the person who may achieve it. Francis developed his idea of ecumenism as a polyhedron. The polyhedron is a geometric figure with different angles and lines. All the different parts have their own peculiarity. It's a figure that brings together unity and diversity.

Where does this view of unity come from? In pre-Vatican II Roman Catholic ecumenism, other Christians were urgently invited to 'come back' into the Catholic fold and to conform to its doctrines and practices under the rule of the pope. With Vatican II (1962–5), Roman Catholicism updated its ecumenical project and embraced a 'concentric circle' type of unity in which the one and only church 'subsists in' the Roman Catholic Church, and other churches and communities gravitate around this centre according to their degree of nearness or distance from it. According to Vatican II and subsequent magisterial teachings, Christian unity is threefold, characterized by:

1 professing the same faith;
2 celebrating the same Eucharist (i.e. the Roman Catholic way);
3 being united under the same sacramental ministry in apostolic succession (i.e. under the pope).

How does the polyhedron kind of unity as advocated by Pope Francis fit with this post-Vatican II view of unity? For example, as far as the second mark of unity is concerned, is the pope saying that the sacrificial understanding of the Eucharist and the theology of transubstantiation belong at the centre of Christian unity, or are they particulars that can accommodate differences? Is the pope saying that apostolic succession, which is the basis of the hierarchical structure of the Roman Catholic Church, still part of the centre, or is it a variable that is secondary to Christian unity?

Polyhedrons are fascinating figures and Francis's use of the image of a polyhedron is thought-provoking. However, the problem for Christian unity does not primarily lie in the metaphors used but in the theological vision that nurtures it. If the Catholic Eucharist and the Catholic sacramental system are part of the centre of Christian unity, we can make reference to spheres or polyhedrons all we like, but the substance of the problem still remains. The unity proposed by Francis still gravitates around the Roman Catholic Church and its distinct outlook, and not around the biblical gospel that calls all Christians to conform to the mind of Christ.

Closer to all?

Francis's ecumenical initiatives are based more on personal contacts with leaders of different churches and organizations than on institutional channels. In performing his role, the pope does not totally depend on Vatican bureaucracy but instead retains his own sphere of initiative. This relational aspect is often underlined as the primary way to foster mutual trust and deeper relationships. In Francis's view, theological dialogues are less important than personal acquaintances. Nothing changes as far as the long-term goal is concerned – namely the pope presiding over the whole Christian church – but this is not the issue that the pope likes to focus on. The important thing for him is to say that we are friends, brothers, sisters, already 'one' in some sense.

Francis wants different ecumenical partners and friends to be valued, listened to, cared for and even admired. He wants to affirm them and wants them to feel appreciated. Theological and ecclesiastical alignments are secondary. Anyone interested in what is happening with this pope should note that the paradigm he is operating under is that of an ecumenism of friendship rather than one of convictions. The two are not opposed, but the emphasis for him lies on the former, not the latter.

Another impressive mark of Pope Francis's ecumenism is that he manages to get closer to all his ecumenical partners without making distinctions between them. He has similar words, attitudes and approaches to Eastern Orthodox of various stripes, liberal Protestants, Anglicans, evangelicals, Pentecostals and other kinds of Christians. Theologically speaking, this is rather awkward because the closer you get to the sacramentalism and the devotions of the East, the further away you go from the liberal agenda of most

Western Protestant churches, and vice versa. Furthermore, as you draw nearer to the 'free' church tradition of Pentecostalism, you at the same time distance yourself from the highly hierarchical and sacramental ecclesiology of both the Roman and the Eastern traditions. But this is not so for Pope Francis. As already pointed out, this is not his approach. Instead, he invests in relationships with all people while leaving aside theological traditions and ecclesiastical settlements. He wants to get closer to all.

As he draws nearer to all Christians, Pope Francis is also determined to draw nearer to all people, be they religious or secular. The same brotherly and appreciative afflatus is what marks the pope's attitude towards Jews, Muslims and agnostic intellectuals. Divisive issues are left aside whereas the 'brotherly' dimension is always in the foreground. The pope is clearly pushing with the same intensity the relational side of ecumenism and interreligious dialogue as if they were two intertwined paths to achieving the overall catholic goal: the Catholic Church as 'a sacrament or as a sign and instrument both of a very closely knit union with God and of the unity of the whole human race' (*LG* 1). The goal of Rome is to recapitulate the whole world into its fold.

In talking about unity, Francis is open to all, be they Christians or non-Christians, religious or secular people. He calls Muslims brothers and sisters. He prays with them, saying that they are praying to the same God. To secular people he says to follow their conscience and they will be fine. Evangelicals are just one piece in his vision. Unity, like a polyhedron, means that there are different ways to relate to the Catholic Church, but Rome maintains centre stage.

All Brothers

Francis's interplay between mission and unity is evident in his 2020 encyclical *All Brothers*.[27] In it there is an understandable anxiety aimed at dissolving conflicts, overcoming injustices and stopping wars. This concern is commendable, even if the analyses and proposals are political, and therefore can be legitimately discussed.

---

27 <www.vatican.va/content/francesco/en/encyclicals/documents/papa-francesco_20201003_enciclica-fratelli-tutti.html>

What is problematic is the theological key chosen to overcome divisions: the declaration of human fraternity in the name of the divine sonship of all humanity. The pope uses a theological category ('all brothers as all children of God') to create the conditions for a better world.

What are the theological implications of such a statement? Here are a few. First, *All Brothers* raises a soteriological question. If we are all brothers and sisters because we are all children of God, does this mean that all will be saved? The whole encyclical is pervaded by a powerful universalist inspiration that also includes atheists (n. 281). Religions in the broad sense are always presented in a positive sense (nn. 277–279) and there is no mention of a biblical criticism of religions nor of the need for repentance and faith in Jesus Christ as the key to receiving salvation. Everything in the encyclical suggests that everyone, as brothers and sisters, will be saved.

Then there is a Christological issue. Even though Jesus Christ is referred to here and there, his exclusive and 'offensive' claims are kept silent. Francis carefully presents Jesus Christ not as the 'cornerstone' on which the whole building of life stands or collapses, but as a rock only for those who recognize him. Above Jesus Christ, according to the encyclical, there is a 'God' who is the father of all. We are children of this 'God' even without recognizing Jesus Christ as Lord and Saviour. Jesus is thus reduced to the rank of the champion of Christians alone, while the other 'brothers' are still children of the same 'God' regardless of faith in Jesus Christ.

Third, there is an ecclesiological issue. If we are all 'brothers', there is a sense in which we are all part of the same church that gathers brothers and sisters together. The boundaries between humanity and church are so non-existent that the two communities become coincident. Humanity is the church and the church is humanity. This is in line with the sacramental vision of the Roman Catholic Church which, according to Vatican II, is understood as a 'sign and instrument of the unity of the whole human race' (*LG* 1). According to the encyclical, the whole of the human race belongs to the church not on the basis of faith in Jesus Christ but on the basis of general kinship and a shared status as children of God.

The theological cost of *All Brothers* is enormous. The message that it sends is eternally devastating. The public inside and outside the Roman Catholic Church will see the consolidation of the idea that God ultimately saves everyone, that Jesus Christ is one among many, and that the church is inclusive of all on the basis of a common and shared humanity, not on the basis of repentance and faith in Jesus Christ. This is *not* the gospel of Jesus Christ.

After the Council of Trent (1545–63) and up to Vatican II (1962–5), Roman Catholicism related to 'others' (be they Protestants, adherents of other religions, or members of different cultural and social movements) through its 'Roman' claims and called them to return to the fold. Only Roman Catholics in communion with the Roman pope were 'brothers'. The others were 'pagans', 'heretics' and 'schismatics' – those excluded from sacramental grace, which is accessible only through the hierarchical system of the Roman Catholic Church. With Vatican II, it was Rome's 'catholicity' that prevailed over its 'Roman' centredness. Protestants have become 'separated brethren', other religions have been viewed positively and people in general have been approached as 'anonymous Christians'. Now, according to Francis's encyclical, we are 'all brothers'. The expansion of catholicity has been further stretched. From being excluded from the 'Roman' side of Rome, we are now all included in the 'catholic' side of Rome.

Unity among believers

Unity needs a more biblical foundation than that described above.[28] Rather than being granted through baptism or being maintained within a human institution, unity is a gift given to believers in Jesus Christ. According to the first letter of Peter, unity is a privilege of those who, having been elected by the Father and sanctified by the Spirit, obey the Son Jesus Christ (1:1–2). They are born again (1:3) and saved (1:5), waiting for their heavenly inheritance (1:4). These are people to whom faith has been granted and in whom that faith is now tested (1:7). This people which responded in faith to God's

---

28 For a fresh presentation of the biblical criteria for unity, see J. Lamb, *Essentially One: Striving for the unity God loves* (London: IVP, 2020).

initiative is 'a chosen race, a royal priesthood, a holy nation, a people for his own possession' (1 Pet. 2:9). In other words, unity is a corollary of the gift of salvation in Jesus Christ which is granted to those who believe in him.

The ecumenical view of unity – to which Roman Catholicism adheres – posits the foundation of unity in the sacrament of baptism. But this view is biblically wrong. There is a far better way to appreciate and to celebrate Christian unity. It is the unity found among believers in Jesus Christ, that is, people who have made a public profession of their faith in the Jesus of the Bible. It is with fellow believers only that Christians can join in prayer asking God to help them 'to maintain the unity of the Spirit' (Eph. 4:3). Unity is based on the truth of the Word of God (John 17:16) and is aimed at witnessing to the world (17:21). The visibility of this unity, as important as it is, depends on the spiritual reality which is a reflection of the trinitarian life and is above all a gift for believers in Jesus Christ so that others too might come to him. It is primarily unseen and internal, although it manifests itself visibly. The trinitarian foundation speaks about the depth and scope of this union, but it does not spell out any given institutional path in which it is bound to express itself.[29]

The final goal of Roman Catholic ecumenism is to have the whole church and the whole world *cum Petro* (with Peter, i.e. in fellowship with the pope) and *sub Petro* (under Peter, i.e. in submission to the pope). For biblical unity to be expressed, however, neither a particular form of apostolic succession nor a particular sacramental and hierarchical system can be derived from the Trinity itself, as if it were the pattern for Christian unity. On top of being founded on a faulty biblical basis, Rome's view of unity also has a this-worldly, political overtone that makes it different from the unity Jesus prayed for and gave his life to achieve.

---

29 The two biblical foundational texts on unity (John 17 and Eph. 4) are expounded by D. M. Lloyd-Jones, *The Basis of Christian Unity: An exposition of John 17 and Ephesians 4* (London: Inter-Varsity Press, 1962).

3

Key Roman Catholic word contents: digging into specific terms

While there are words that are associated with the Christian faith generally and are used by Christians of all stripes and traditions, there are other terms which are unique to and particular indicators of the Roman Catholic faith. In this chapter some of these specifically Roman Catholic words will be briefly presented and biblically assessed.

A particular distinctive of Roman Catholicism is of course the papacy, as we have already seen, though there are other areas of divergence. When we think of the papacy our attention is immediately drawn to a defining institution of the Roman Catholic establishment which is embedded in its theological vision. When we refer to the realm of Mariology we enter a world that – while not being excusively Roman Catholic – is nonetheless primarily attached to the Roman Catholic faith and its practice. Moreover, especially those who have a background in Protestantism will soon recognize the importance of indulgences in the sixteenth-century debates that gave rise to the Reformation and how indulgences are still offered in that they belong to the Roman Catholic teaching on salvation, the church and the afterlife.

Papacy

The *Catechism of the Catholic Church* states, 'The Roman Pontiff, by reason of his office as Vicar of Christ, and as pastor of the entire Church has full, supreme, and universal power over the whole

70

Church, a power which he can always exercise unhindered' (882). Further reinforcing his power and authority, the *Catechism* claims, 'The Pope enjoys, by divine institution, supreme, full, immediate, and universal power in the care of souls' (937). The *Catechism* presents the papacy as a divinely appointed institution that presides over the life of the church and exercises its rule over God's flock.

Where do these massive claims come from? Roman Catholics trace the pope's origin to the apostle Peter. But history tells a different story.[1]

On what rock?

Rome wasn't built in a day, and neither was the Roman Catholic papacy. It was a long process that led to the setting up of this millennia-old office that combines spiritual and political power claims.

The pope claims to hold an office originally bestowed by Jesus on the apostle Peter, and one which has been passed down through a direct and unbroken line of succeeding apostles. In other words, the pope claims to hold apostolic authority and continue the mission Jesus supposedly entrusted to Peter in Matthew 16:18: 'You are Peter, and on this rock I will build my church.'

The Roman Catholic Church sees an embryonic stage of the papacy in this passage. It believes Jesus gave to Peter (and, by implication, to all his formal successors) a foundational role in the building of his church. Subsequent traditions and practices continued to develop the bishop of Rome's role to the point at which the papacy eventually emerged.

However, when we do a little digging, we soon enough find no meaningful connection between what Jesus says of Peter in Matthew 16:18 and the function of the papacy. The pope claims a succession to Peter's ministry, but Jesus makes no reference to such a succession. Nor can we see in the text how this succession became attributed to the city of Rome, or find any clue to the imperial form that the papacy took.

---

1   A more extensive treatment can be found in my book *A Christian's Pocket Guide to the Papacy: Its origin and role in the 21st century* (Fearn: Christian Focus, 2015).

A better interpretation of Matthew 16:18 is that the church, the community of Jesus' disciples, will be built on Peter's *confession of faith* that Jesus is the Christ, the Son of the living God, not on Peter himself. Jesus underlines the fact by saying that 'my' church will be built in such a way. It is not Peter's church; it is the church of Jesus, founded by Jesus as the Messiah. Jesus is the founder and the builder of the church, whereas Peter is a witness, a spokesperson of this divine truth that God was revealing to him and the other disciples.

Moreover, Jesus gives no indication that Peter will have successors that will take his place. This text can be seen as the biblical basis for the papacy only if the doctrine of the papacy has already been established apart from Scripture, and then subsequently and retrospectively squeezed into it.

Child of the empire

If the papacy isn't the office of Peter's apostolic successors, where did it come from? A look at history shows that it is far more a product of the Roman Empire than of Peter's ministry. The Roman imperial pattern was the influential blueprint that shaped the papal institution from the fourth century onwards. The papacy is more a child of imperial categories than of biblical ones. The papacy never would have emerged if there were no empire forming the political and cultural milieu of the life of the early church.

The slow process that led to the formation of the papacy depended on the importance of Rome as the capital city of the empire and on the power it exercised in the ancient world. The ideology of *Roma aeterna* (eternal Rome) crept into the church and influenced the way Christians perceived the role of the Church of Rome in relation to the role of the city in the affairs of the empire.

As the Roman Empire gradually abandoned the West, what was left in Rome was the 'imperial' structure of the church with the pope as its head. Then, between the fourth and fifth centuries, popes applied to themselves the title of *pontifex*, the name of the chief high priest in ancient Rome.

Several centuries later, confronted with the Protestant Reformation, which invited the church to turn from its self-absorption and rediscover the gospel of God's grace, Rome strengthened the sacramental system that made the church the mediator of divine grace. Then, confronted with modernity, which pushed for a review of the prerogatives of the church over society and people's consciences, Rome elevated the papacy to an even more accentuated role through the dogma of papal infallibility – a move without any biblical support whatsoever.

Rome versus the Reformers

The papacy is a child of the Roman institutional church, rather than a child of Scripture. This is why the Protestant Reformers took issue with it. In writing against the Catholic theologian Johannes Eck in 1519, Martin Luther developed his critical approach towards the papacy with a full set of arguments.

According to the German Reformer, the authority of popes and councils should be subordinate to that of the Bible. The papacy was not instituted by Christ but was instead established by the church over the course of its history. So it does not come from 'divine law' but is instead a human institution.

Luther argued, further, that the 'rock' of Matthew 16:18 is not a reference to Peter but is either his confession of Jesus on behalf of the whole church or a description of Christ himself. Christ alone is the solid foundation of the church (1 Cor. 3:11). The Roman popes have nothing 'Petrine' about them, nor is there anything 'papal' in Peter. The papacy is not commanded or foreseen in Scripture, and therefore obedience to the Word of God must take precedence over obedience to any mere human. Luther stressed that if the pope disobeys Scripture, the faithful Christian should follow the latter without hesitation. Christians are not obligated to obey an unfaithful pope.

In 1544, writing on the unity of the church, John Calvin also refuted Catholic arguments for the papacy, stating that while Scripture often speaks of Christ as the head of the church, it never speaks of the pope this way. The unity of the church is based on one God, one faith and one baptism (Eph. 4:4–5), with no mention of the necessity of the pope in order for the church to be the church.

Moreover, Calvin argued, the apostle Paul, in listing the ministries and offices of the church, is silent about a present or future papacy. Peter was Paul's co-worker, not his pope-like leader. The universal bishop of the church is Christ alone.

To this biblical argument for the headship of Christ, Calvin added a historical reference to some patristic writings that support the same New Testament view. Even Cyprian of Carthage, a Church Father considered by many to have favoured an early form of the papacy, calls the bishop of Rome a 'brother, and colleague in the episcopate', thus showing that he did not have in view the kind of primacy that was later attributed to the pope.[2]

To keep the unity of the church, Christ alone is the Lord we need. This was true in the sixteenth century and it continues to be true today.

Papal infallibility?

The First Vatican Council (1869–70) provided the most comprehensive and authoritative doctrinal statement on the papacy in the modern era.[3] Instead of taking into account the biblical challenges legitimately offered by the Protestant Reformation, and instead of listening to certain trends of modern thought that advocated freedom of conscience and freedom of religion, Vatican I further solidified the nature of the papal office as that of a quasi-omnipotent and infallible figure. The Roman Catholic Church invested its highest doctrinal authority, namely the promulgation of a dogma – a binding, irreversible, unchangeable truth – to cement the institution of the papacy by furthering its absolute nature.

Vatican I restricts the pope's infallibility to those occasions when he speaks *ex cathedra* (with the full authority of office; literally, from the chair). The question is: when did he speak in such a way? What are the papal pronouncements – among the dozens of nineteenth- and twentieth-century papal encyclicals and documents – that are endowed with the 'infallibility' that the document *Pastor Aeternus*

---

2 <www.newadvent.org/fathers/050671.htm>
3 See J. O'Malley, *Vatican I: The council and the making of the ultramontane church* (Cambridge, MA: The Belknap Press, 2018).

grants to the pope? Even in Catholic theological circles the issue of the extension of infallibility is debated.

Logically speaking, *Pastor Aeternus* must be one of these pronouncements. The papal document defining papal infallibility must be considered infallible; otherwise the whole argument undergirding it collapses.

While there might be different opinions about the exercise of infallibility, there is at least one clear example of a subsequent papal teaching that Roman Catholics must take as infallible.

It was in 1950 that Pius XII issued the dogma of the bodily assumption of Mary as a binding belief for the Roman Catholic faith. With the dogmatic constitution *Munificentissimus Deus*, Rome committed to it: 'We pronounce, declare, and define it to be a divinely revealed dogma: that the Immaculate Mother of God, the ever Virgin Mary, having completed the course of her earthly life, was assumed body and soul into heavenly glory' (n. 44). This is clearly the formula of an infallible, *ex cathedra* statement. No Roman Catholic theologian can question it. In passing, let us note that the Bible is not interested in the final days of Mary nor in the way she died. She must have died like anyone else, and yet here we are confronted not with an opinion but with a dogma. The Roman Catholic Church invested its highest magisterial authority to formulate a belief which the Scriptures are silent on, to say the least.

On the basis of a non-biblical dogma, namely the pope's infallibility, another non-biblical dogma, namely Mary's assumption, was constructed, thus becoming part of the binding and irreformable teaching of the Roman Catholic Church. Biblically speaking, one could say: from bad to worse; but this is what Rome is committed to and will continue to be committed to, in spite of all 'ecumenical' developments and friendlier attitudes. The flawed Roman Catholic theological system operates in this way: not reforming what is contrary to Scripture but rather consolidating it with other non-biblical doctrines and practices. After 150 years since Vatican I, the only hope for change is a reformation according to the biblical gospel that will question and ultimately dismantle and reject papal infallibility.

What about the world?

In today's society, the notion of papal infallibility is only one side of the matter. In ecumenical circles, many are inclined to believe that, in our interconnected world, a global Christian spokesperson would be practically useful for Christianity as a whole. In interfaith circles, some religious leaders (for example, from the Muslim community) go so far as to say that the pope represents the whole of humanity when he advocates for the poor of the world or when he makes appeals for peace.

The world, both religious and secular, seems to yearn for a global figure to provide leadership, but no political institution and no international organization seems able to provide such an individual at the moment. Therefore, Protestants are pressed with the question: does humankind need a leader in order to live in peace? It's a question that continues to be posed to Bible-believing Christians, especially in times when the pope attracts much attention and is looked at as being one of the few, if not the only one, who can speak on behalf of all.

The troublesome reality, however, is that the pope continues to claim religious and political roles that are biblically unwarranted. As the church does not need a mere human pope to be united, so the world does not need a global religious leader, other than Christ himself, to live in peace. Jesus said, 'Peace I leave with you; my peace I give to you' (John 14:27). The church and the world need Jesus Christ, and him alone.

Mary

The simple sound of the name 'Mary' opens up very different scenarios in different people's hearts and minds.[4] For most evangelical Protestants, she is who the New Testament says she is: a young Jewish woman who was chosen by God to supernaturally conceive and give birth to Jesus, thus being part of the way in which the Son

---

4   For more on the subject of this section see my book *A Christian's Pocket Guide to Mary: Mother of God?* (Fearn: Christian Focus, 2017).

of God became a man. Part of this biblical portrayal indicates that she was also a member of the first community of men and women who followed Jesus, and not without doubts and setbacks. She is soberly respected yet not occupying centre stage in their overall Christian experience. For many Roman Catholics, however, Mary deeply shapes their whole spirituality and entire life. She is prayed to, and is a venerated person surrounded by a vast array of 'Marian' devotions (e.g. rosaries, processions, pilgrimages). The titles with which she is honoured (e.g. Heavenly Queen, Mediatrix, Advocate) resemble those ascribed to her Son Jesus Christ. She looks like an altogether different person from the one she was perceived to be by the previous group.

Mary or Mariology?

The Mary of Roman Catholicism is no longer the Mary of the Bible. Rome has its own Mariology, namely the doctrine of Mary, but has lost the biblical Mary. Mariology is the theme of two recently promulgated dogmas (i.e. binding beliefs): the 1854 dogma of the immaculate conception and the 1950 dogma of the bodily assumption into heaven. Mariology impinges not only on the doctrine of revelation (the whole Mariological doctrine is founded on tradition rather than the Bible) but also on the doctrine of the Trinity (she receives prayers and petitions, obscuring the work of Christ and the Spirit), salvation (she has a role in the work of salvation) and so on. In nations and cultures dominated by Roman Catholicism, intertwined with lofty dogmatic definitions, it is the practice of devotional and popular Marianism that largely defines the religious experience of many Roman Catholic faithful who pray to her and are devoutly committed to her. The *Catechism of the Catholic Church* goes so far as to say that 'the Church's devotion to the Blessed Virgin is intrinsic to Christian worship' (971). To say it is 'intrinsic' means that it is inherent to Christian worship; there can be no proper worship without the devotion to Mary. It also implies that when dealing with Marian devotion, one touches a central nerve of the whole of Roman Catholic spirituality, not something that can be dealt with independently. This is a feature, not a bug, as some might say.

Prayer to Mary is what quintessentially defines Marian spirituality. Mary is perhaps the most invoked figure in many religious quarters. She is acclaimed as mother and is movingly sought to provide help and strength. She is eminently given veneration and is approached with reverence and awe. Mary can be approached confidently because she can obtain for us from her divine Son anything she asks for. Against the background of such deep theological and devotional vision, the list of Roman Catholic prayers mirrors a Marian-centred spirituality; 'Hail, Holy Queen', 'Regina Coeli' (Queen of Heaven) and 'Ave Maris Stella' (Hail, Star of the Ocean) are only a few of the most common and popular Marian prayers.

Another significant form of Marian prayer is related to the rosary. The word 'rosary' means 'crown of roses'. The conviction behind this expression is that Mary has revealed to several people that each time someone says a 'Hail Mary' prayer, he or she is giving her a rose, and that each complete rosary makes her a crown of roses. The Holy Rosary is considered a perfect prayer because within it lies the awesome story of salvation retold in a way that highlights Mary's central role in redemption. Instead of inculcating salvation history as the Bible tells it, the rosary is a powerful tool to shape one's own imagination in terms of the pervasive presence and agency of Mary in whatever the triune God is and does. The whole orientation of Roman Catholic 'biblical theology' is inherently Marian in that Mary is thought of as sharing the prerogatives and roles of the Son.

Marian shrines and apparitions

Apart from shaping the life of prayer and the overall spiritual under-standing of salvation history, Mariology is also a determining factor in arranging Christian worship in its spatial dimension. Thousands of church buildings around the world are dedicated to Mary, thus forging visually and materialistically the minds and hearts of mil-lions of people. The religious arts have also significantly developed along a uniquely Marian track, becoming an integral part of the Christian imagination. Beside huge churches and sanctuaries, Marian devotion marks its territory in the form of small shrines disseminated in many areas – for example at crossroads, and in hospitals, schools, apartment blocks and offices – so as to signify the nearness of Mary in everyday life and in every place.

The strong Marian emphasis of Roman Catholicism has also been enriched by alleged apparitions of Mary across the centuries, with an increase of these episodes since the nineteenth century when Marian piety pushed the church to promulgate the dogma of Mary's immaculate conception (1854). Each apparition has generated the rise of more devotional practices, such as pilgrimages and the building of shrines to cultivate the memory of the apparition and to further its message. The most famous Marian apparitions are those associated with Guadalupe (Mexico), Lourdes (France) and Fatima (Portugal). Rather than promoting a Bible-based and Christ-centred faith, all these messages have reinforced Marian practices and venerations. While Marian apparitions may at times seem like fanciful tales to non-Catholic observers, their impact has been significant. They have led to the conversion of millions of people to Roman Catholicism, the building of some of the largest Marian shrines around the world, the formation of Marian movements dedicated to the spreading of Marian devotions, the encouragement given to the development of Mariological doctrines and the drawing of hundreds of millions of people to Marian sites on pilgrimage.

How central is Mariology?

In all its theological force and devotional ramifications, Mariology is an inescapable, all-embracing and fundamental tenet of Roman Catholic theology and practice. For many Bible-believing Christians, Mariology is a big source of puzzlement. They love Mary, but it is difficult to see her in the expanded universe of Mariology and Marian devotions. They cannot come to terms with what happened to the memory of this young woman, called by God the Father to be the bearer of the person of the Lord Jesus, after the end of the apostolic age and especially from the fifth century onwards. They don't see how the biblical Mary can be reconciled with the hyper-trophic Mary of subsequent Mariology. Its development seems to respond to rules and criteria that go way beyond what is written in the Bible.

The bodily assumption of Mary was the last non-biblical dogma of the Roman Catholic Church in chronological order. Some sectors within Roman Catholicism are pushing for it not to be the last in the definitive sense. For several decades, the dogma of Mary being 'co-redemptrix' has been on the horizon, a further development of the ancient Marian syllogism according to which everything that is ascribed to Jesus Christ must in some way also be ascribed to Mary.

This syllogism resulted in two Marian dogmas:

- since Jesus is sinless, Mary ought to be believed to have been conceived without sin (i.e. the 1854 dogma of the immaculate conception of Mary);
- since Jesus rose from the dead, Mary ought to be believed to have been assumed into heavenly glory (i.e. the 1950 dogma of her bodily assumption).

The 'logic' of the uncontrolled syllogism would have it that, since Jesus Christ is the Redeemer of the world, Mary is 'co-redemptrix', having shared and still sharing her role in the salvation brought by the Son. Such a conclusion would be the apotheosis of an 'unthinkable' theological mechanism that has already produced two non-biblical and deviant dogmas. The 'co-redemptrix' dogma has been brewing for some time; it may take ages to come to the forefront, but it is definitely emerging.

While the outspoken intention of Roman Catholic Mariology is that Mariological doctrines and Marian practices in no way divert attention from Jesus Christ, the reality is that the line Rome wishes to preserve is indeed crossed in multiple ways. When entire shrines or processions or prayer chains are dedicated to Mary so as to completely shape the devotees' lives, one finds it hard to attribute it simply to the devotional excesses of poorly informed popular piety. Separating Christian worship duly expressed from cultish practices fraught with paganism is a soft, even liquid borderline that is not sufficiently maintained and safeguarded, despite the good intentions expressed in the church's official teaching. The question is whether or not Mariology as it currently stands, with its dogmatic outlook and devotional pervasiveness, involves an inherent proximity to, if not blurring with, a form of worship which is not biblically defendable. The indisputable evidence of many of these devotional acts and habits indicates that in many people's lives the centrality of Mary is experienced much more than reverence and obedience to Christ. All this happens not *in spite of* what the Roman Catholic Church teaches but *because of* what it explicitly or implicitly endorses. The Mary of Rome, although carrying the same name, is not the Mary of the Bible.

Mercy and indulgences

If we want to understand Pope Francis and a major present-day trend in the Roman Catholic Church, we need to come to terms with the word 'mercy'. 'Mercy', of course, is a wonderful biblical term referring to one aspect of the character of God: being generous, kind and patient. According to Scripture, Christ is the 'merciful and faithful high priest' who made 'propitiation for the sins of the people' (Heb. 2:17). Any biblical understanding of mercy needs to be interwoven with God's justice and with Christ's atonement which calls for repentance and faith. Otherwise, mercy can be (ab)used as a general manifestation of kindness which does not depict God's mercy at all but is rather a form of humanistic goodwill. In the Roman Catholic understanding, especially as it applies to Pope Francis, this is what actually happens.

Jubilee of mercy?

Pope Francis surprised the Catholic community and the public by unexpectedly announcing the indiction of an extraordinary jubilee year beginning at the end of 2015 and running throughout most of 2016. The tradition of celebrating jubilee years dates back to AD 1300 when Pope Boniface VIII issued the first holy year, calling pilgrims to visit Rome in order to receive a plenary indulgence. The name 'jubilee' reminds us of the biblical institution of the jubilee whereby, according to the Mosaic law, every fifty years slaves were supposed to be freed and debts had to be cancelled (e.g. Lev. 25). However, in spite of the name, the Roman ecclesiastical jubilee has little to do with this biblical precedent; it is mostly to do with the medieval practice of a powerful church granting remission of the penalty of sin by shortening the time people would spend in purgatory. The Vatican jubilee was therefore part and parcel of a theological vision whereby purgatory is a pillar of the afterlife, the church claims to administer God's grace on his behalf, and pilgrims have to do some penitential acts like reciting rosaries, making pilgrimages and fasting, that is, performing religious works, in order to receive the remission. It is not a coincidence that Martin Luther, after visiting Rome in 1511, became troubled about the practice of indulgences and eventually nailed his ninety-five theses to the door of Wittenberg's Castle Church in the (vain) hope that a biblical and public discussion could be initiated.

Francis wanted his jubilee year to be focused on mercy. The overall theme of the year and of its wide-ranging activities was mercy. This is not a new emphasis. His 2013 apostolic exhortation *Evangelii Gaudium* (The Joy of the Gospel) had already centred on mercy as an encompassing rubric of the mission of the church. After being elected, Francis went public in saying that he was reading a book by Cardinal Walter Kasper on mercy and that he was profoundly impressed by it.[5] So, the Jubilee of Mercy was to be a vantage point from which Francis's understanding of mercy could be displayed in full force.

So far, some indications about how the current pope understands mercy are a mixed bag. In the first two years of his reign, mercy was often swollen with regard to its biblical meaning in such a way as to refer to a sort of divine and universal benevolence towards all. Eye-catching sentences like 'Who am I to judge?', 'God forgives those who follow their conscience' and 'God always forgives' contributed to widening God's mercy to the point of being exchanged for an all-embracing, all-inclusive love.

---

5   W. Kasper, *Mercy: The essence of the gospel and the key to Christian life* (Mahwah, NJ: Paulist Press, 2014).

What about indulgences?

The bull of indiction of the Jubilee of Mercy was issued on 11 April 2015 and is entitled *Misericordiae Vultus* (The Face of Mercy).[6] There was some curiosity about how this outward-looking pope who comes 'from the ends of the world' would treat a very 'Roman' and ecclesiastical topic like indulgences. The answer is found in paragraphs 21–22 where Pope Francis uses a form of language much more personal and relational than juridical and traditional, yet the substance of the theology and practice of the indulgences is granted.

'Mercy' is by far the word most commonly used by Pope Francis. Arguably, it is the interpretative key of his whole pontificate. The book on mercy by Cardinal Kasper (mentioned above) was on his bedside table when he was elected pope, thus shaping his own personal reflections as he prepared to become pontiff. Mercy was the main rubric of the Synod of the Family when the pope urged his church to apply less rigorously the 'letter' of the teachings on sexuality and to listen more to the 'spirit' of inclusion for those who live in various forms of irregular relationships. Mercy is the over-arching theme of the jubilee year which Francis indicted in order to offer a year-long display of mercy through the system of indulgences. It is not surprising, therefore, that mercy is also the main theme of his more recent speeches where he expounded it and unfolded it. The following instance was the general audience given on 3 February 2016 in Saint Peter's Square in Rome.[7]

Mercy and justice

The vexed question of the relationship between mercy and justice is central to the pope's meditation. Here is how he sets the tone of it: 'Sacred Scripture presents God to us as infinite mercy and as perfect justice. How do we reconcile the two?' There seems to be a

---

6 <www.vatican.va/content/francesco/en/apost_letters/documents/papa-francesco_bolla_20150411_misericordiae-vultus.html>
7 The full text can be found here: <www.vatican.va/content/francesco/en/audiences/2016/documents/papa-francesco_20160203_udienza-generale.html>

contradiction between God's mercy and God's justice. One way of connecting mercy and justice is through 'retributive justice' which 'inflicts a penalty on the guilty party, according to the principle that each person must be given his or her due'. Justice is done when a person receives what is owed to him or her. Francis makes reference to a couple of Bible verses that show retributive justice at work, but he wants to challenge it: 'This path does not lead to true justice because in reality it does not conquer evil, it merely checks it. Only by responding to it with good can evil be truly overcome.' The unnecessary implication here is that retributive justice never produces any good. Does it not?

There is a far better way of doing justice according to Francis:

> It is a process that avoids recourse to the tribunal and allows the victim to face the culprit directly and invite him or her to conversion, helping the person to understand that they are doing evil, thus appealing to their conscience. And this is beautiful: after being persuaded that what was done was wrong, the heart opens to the forgiveness being offered to it. This is the way to resolve conflicts in the family, in the relationship between spouses or between parents and children, where the offended party loves the guilty one and wishes to save the bond that unites them.

According to the pope, mercy achieves justice by avoiding tribunals, sentences and prices to be paid. A whole chunk of what the Bible teaches on justice is chopped out and replaced by a merciful and atonement-less justice. Is this God's justice though?

This is God's paradigm of mercy, says Francis. 'This is how God acts towards us sinners. The Lord continually offers us his pardon and helps us to accept it and to be aware of our wrongdoing so as to free us of it.' What is happening here? No reference is made to the cross, the penalty of sin that was paid there, the wonder of Jesus Christ being punished on our behalf, the need for repentance and conversion for those who believe. Mercy seems to relinquish the cross. The point is that biblical atonement is totally missing here, and the resulting view of mercy and justice is severely flawed.

What about atonement?

Unfortunately, the pope's teaching above is a seriously faulty teaching. Atonement-free justice is one of the popular ways to reimagine God's dealings with sin which is practised by significant thinkers in contemporary theology. Anything that sounds connected to punishment, carried out in execution of a lawful sentence, objectively imparted, and so on, is seen as belonging to an old-fashioned, patriarchal, legalistic understanding of justice that needs to be overcome by a merciful, restorative, loving extension of pardon. In other words, what contemporary theology seems to reject are the basics of covenant justice instituted by the covenant God of Scripture. This justice presents a righteous Father who is also love, who sent his Son, the God-man Jesus, to pay for sin in order to bring salvation. Fulfilling the Old Testament, Jesus is the Lamb of God who takes away the sin of the world (John 1:29). Through his sacrifice, he is God's provision for the forgiveness of sin.

Biblical justice has the cross of Christ at the centre (1 Cor. 1:23): Jesus Christ bore our sin on the cross (1 Pet. 2:24). Mercy is possible not because tribunals and sentences are left out and made redundant by an all-embracing love. Mercy is accomplished and displayed exactly because justice was satisfied: 'without the shedding of blood there is no forgiveness of sins' (Heb. 9:22). This was accomplished not by us, but by our Substitute, Jesus Christ, who died on the cross for us (Rom. 5:8). When Pope Francis speaks of mercy, is he missing this fundamental biblical truth?

In closing, we note that almost overlapping with the Jubilee of Mercy was the fifth centenary of the Protestant Reformation in 2017. It is interesting to observe that while on the one hand the Roman Catholic Church was officially preparing an 'ecumenical' commemoration of the Reformation, on the other it represented and promoted again the theology and the practice that caused the Reformation, namely the granting of indulgences. How is it possible to commemorate something that was opposed to the indulgences and, at the same time, focus on the same theological framework that was the cause of the dispute? Is it because the Roman Church is, despite all change, *semper eadem*, always the same?

4

The Roman Catholic world: connecting its words, investigating its core

The religious vocabulary of Roman Catholicism contains several words that stem from biblical language. They form the backbone of an account of the Christian faith which appears to be faithful to Scripture and which carries the particular Roman Catholic flavour. As we have seen from the brief analysis of some key words, however, the reality beneath the surface is very different. Their meaning, though partially shaped by biblical content, is also largely influenced by other elements that do not belong to the biblical message. Moreover, the Roman Catholic 'logic' through which they are connected and make sense as a whole is indebted to theological principles and devotional practices that have developed over the centuries and that have lost sight of the biblical matrix of the Christian faith. The overall result is that while using the words of the Bible, Roman Catholicism fails to be a coherent and faithful biblical faith. It resembles such a faith, it sounds like a version of it, it looks like a legitimate variation of it, but it departs from it at crucial junctures, resulting in a blurred, flawed, confused and confusing form of Christianity. There is something intrinsic and deeply woven into its fabric that shapes it and makes it different from the 'faith that was once for all delivered to the saints' (Jude 3). The problem of Roman Catholicism lies not so much in its components as in the theological DNA which informs and moulds all of its parts.

After surveying some important words of Roman Catholicism, the focus needs to be the exploration of its theological world. This chapter will attempt to sketch the theological framework that makes

Roman Catholicism what it is, giving meaning to its words, accounting for its structures, promoting its practices and fuelling its mission. In order to account for it, one needs to see the 'big picture' and to approach Roman Catholicism as a whole.

Decoding present-day Roman Catholicism

Approaching Roman Catholicism has often been a daunting experience for evangelicals, especially in its present-day manifestation. While encountering post-Vatican II Rome, evangelicals are puzzled to find the restatement of traditional Roman Catholic teaching together with something that appears to contradict it. The chief example of the evangelical puzzlement is David Wells's book *Revolution in Rome* (1972) where he attempts to make sense of the nuanced, juxtaposing and cumulative ways of theologizing characteristic of Vatican II.[1] After carefully reading its documents, Wells concludes that Vatican II on some strategic points (e.g. authority, ecumenism, religious freedom, the presence of the church in the world) seems to endorse 'mutually incompatible theologies', one conservative, the other progressive; one restating tradition, the other pushing beyond tradition. 'How do we interpret this?' is the question that reflects the evangelical perplexity in coming to terms with the complexity of the Roman Catholic mindset as it was presented at Vatican II.

Scores of books have been written on Vatican II, the discussions behind its texts, the documents that were produced and the controversial attempts to implement it. Its legacy is still a fiercely disputed matter in Catholic circles as well. This is to say that each new addition to the Vatican II library is a welcomed attempt at trying to navigate the deep waters of the council. A recent book by Thomas G. Guarino[2] is particularly helpful for evangelicals for at least two reasons. First, since 2009 the author has been co-chairing the US-based

---

1 D. Wells, *Revolution in Rome* (Downers Grove, IL: InterVarsity Press, 1972).
2 T. G. Guarino, *The Disputed Teaching of Vatican II: Continuity and reversal in Catholic doctrine* (Grand Rapids, MI: Eerdmans, 2018).

Evangelicals and Catholics Together initiative and therefore is used to dialogue with evangelicals. Second, while never quoting David Wells, Guarino discusses some of the evangelical perplexities contained in his book with the intention of suggesting a Roman Catholic way to handle them.

Vatican II as *profectus fidei* (a development of the faith)?

The church has always been confronted with the issue of change in its understanding of the truth and its accounting of it in teaching, preaching, evangelizing and so on. This is why Guarino looks back to the fifth century at Vincent of Lérins's distinction between change as *profectus* (i.e. a development of doctrine that preserves the core) and change as *permutatio* (i.e. a mutation that alters the core). Without denying the significant changes in language, style and tone that are evident at the council, Guarino argues that 'Vatican II was in the main a homogeneous *profectus* of the earlier tradition',[3] that is, an advancement and expansion of previous tradition that nonetheless maintained its fundamental landmarks.

The main thesis of the book is that 'Vatican II is in clear congruence with the prior Catholic tradition – even while homogeneously developing it on certain points'.[4] Each word here is important: 'congruence' means compatibility with the past but no mere repetition of it. 'Developing' refers to organic growth, even with points of relative distancing from previous formulations, while remaining faithful to the doctrinal whole. The elastic yet firm combination of continuity and discontinuity at different levels is what characterizes Guarino's appraisal of Vatican II. In borrowing Benedict XVI's terms, instead of a 'hermeneutic of rupture', one needs to come to terms with the meaning of Vatican II by using a 'hermeneutic of reform'.[5] The council witnessed an 'organic, homogeneous, architectonic growth':[6] a kind of change that occurred

---

3 Guarino, *Disputed Teaching*, p. 21.
4 Guarino, *Disputed Teaching*, p. 10.
5 Guarino, *Disputed Teaching*, p. 21.
6 Guarino, *Disputed Teaching*, p. 5.

within the parameters of a coherent development that did not betray the well-established heritage of the church.

This reading of the council is fascinating and in line with a typical Catholic *et–et* (both–and) hermeneutical approach. However, its plausibility is difficult to accept wholesale when, for example, one analyses the evidence as far as the issue of religious freedom is concerned. After centuries of strong opposition to religious freedom and freedom of conscience by Roman Catholic magisterial authorities, after multiple papal encyclicals consistently condemning it (which Guarino fairly makes reference to on pp. 184–188), how is it possible to see in Vatican II's approval of it an 'organic' change that simply 'developed' what had been previously taught? Why not simply say that Rome was wrong when it condemned religious freedom and then came to change its mind at Vatican II? Is it because the institutional church is believed to be indefectible (i.e. not erring or making mistakes)? The fact that the Roman Catholic Church made a U-turn on religious freedom is a clear example showing how the willingness to preserve Rome's continuity goes against the factual evidence. Guarino's overall interpretation of Vatican II as simple *profectus fidei* seems to squeeze the dynamics of the Roman Church into a one-size-fits-all type of approach, instead of accounting for its complexity. Is this not too simplistic and a way to protect the unsustainable claims of indefectibility within the Roman Church?

Three key words

Returning to the central thesis of Guarino's book, there are three key words that one needs to become acquainted with. They are 'development', 'ressourcement' and 'aggiornamento'. These words form the vocabulary that is needed to try to make sense of Vatican II from within. Here is the way in which Guarino helps to clarify their meaning.

Development. Recalling J. H. Newman's famous book *An Essay on the Development of Christian Doctrine* (1894), Guarino acknowledges its profound influence on Vatican II. Development means 'an unfolding of something that is already present implicitly or in germ'.[7] According to Newman and Guarino, doctrine is inherently involved in an organic process of growth. The problem with this Roman Catholic view of development is always the same: what are the biblical boundaries of such a 'development'? For example, can the church develop its Mariology to the point of elevating two Marian dogmas (like the 1854 dogma on Mary's immaculate conception and the 1950 dogma of Mary's bodily assumption) without any biblical support? In other words, 'development' without the biblical principle of *sola scriptura* (i.e. the Bible as the supreme authority for the church) safeguarding and guiding it can become a self-referential principle at the service of the institutional church. If the church can 'develop' its own traditions even outside the perimeter of the written Word of God, is it not a questionable development?

Ressourcement. This word of French origin is another key term for entering the theological universe of Vatican II. It means 'taking account of the entire theological tradition of the church',[8] be it the apostles, the Church Fathers, the councils, the liturgy or the witness of the Christian people. Vatican II is known for having paid attention to the biblical sources of the faith as well as to patristic and liturgical sources. The 'ressourcement' principle is important provided that the examination of the sources and their 'weight' is put under the authority of the Word of God as the supreme source. Vatican II contained more biblical references than previous Catholic documents, but it also stood in continuity with previous magisterial texts that had few scriptural references and were based primarily on *other* sources (e.g. as is the case with the Marian dogmas). Vatican II's ressourcement *added* sources but did not subtract any, even when Rome had developed its theology and practice outside the Bible. It expanded the ability of the Roman Church to absorb new emphases without purifying it of any spurious ones which had been previously embraced.

---

7   Guarino, *Disputed Teaching*, p. 57.
8   Guarino, *Disputed Teaching*, p. 59.

Aggiornamento. The final word that Guarino expounds comes from the Italian language and was used by Pope John XXIII. 'Aggiornamento' means 'bringing up to date'[9] the communication of the church by means of appropriating a different style and tone and making it more attuned to the modern mindset. 'Aggiornamento' can give the impression that at Vatican II Rome really and substantially changed, but it is closer to reality to say that the Roman Church went through a season of updating its language and attitude without relinquishing any of what was previously believed and pronounced. For example, the 'anathemas' (i.e. curses) of the Council of Trent against the Protestants have been 'updated' at Vatican II with a friendly and affectionate form of language but never renounced (and this means that they can be resuscitated at any moment). The previous layer has been updated without being removed.

Guarino's book does an admirable service to the evangelical reader in explaining the Vatican II vocabulary of 'change'. Too often, evangelicals may have a superficial view of the Roman Catholic 'change'. They can be impressed by the emphasis on biblical passages that they find in post-Vatican II documents without properly understanding the fact that these biblical sources *supplement* rather than change the already established Roman Catholic sources which have shaped its teaching. It is also possible that evangelicals might rightly appreciate the friendly tone of present-day Catholic theological language without necessarily knowing that 'aggiornamento' *adds* a new style on top of what Rome has said and done in the past without cutting off its roots. In other words, the vocabulary of Vatican II should not be taken as implying that Rome is now open to a biblical reformation; it simply means that at that council the Catholic Church, as Guarino argues, 'was in continuity with the prior doctrinal landmarks' (read: the Council of Trent, the Marian dogmas, the dogma of papal infallibility), undoubtedly together with some 'true development'[10] that made it more palatable to outsiders. The past is never renounced. It can be updated but remains untouched,

---

9 Guarino, *Disputed Teaching*, p. 66.
10 Guarino, *Disputed Teaching*, p. 199.

and it continues to remain at the core of what the Roman Church is and believes.

A paradigm change

Beyond the already mentioned contributions of Guarino's book to the understanding of Vatican II, this work has yet another strength, perhaps its most important one. In order to assess the theology of Vatican II, its 'theological principles' need to be grappled with and the book helpfully summarizes them. Yes, the 'style' of the council is important (as suggested by J. O'Malley);[11] yes, the key words of the council are foundational ('development', 'ressourcement', 'aggiornamento'); but what about its theological vision? From where did Vatican II derive its principles? And what were they?

Guarino's contention is that 'analogical and participatory thinking are crucial, though generally overlooked, themes at Vatican II'.[12] In his view, analogical and participatory categories form the backbone of the council. Analogical thinking means that similarities are stressed (rather than differences); everything is analogous to something else and therefore close, similar, next to it. Participatory thinking means that everything participates in one way or another in everything else; therefore, mutual indwelling and interrelationships are underlined (rather than distance and separation). If pre-Vatican II Roman Catholicism operated with a 'univocal' approach (i.e. defining reality in one way only) followed by dialectical thinking (i.e. distancing itself from what was not aligned with its univocal definition), at Vatican II Rome learns to reframe its whole theological vision according to what is in common with everything else and what unites it with the rest of the world. 'Dialectical difference was not the style of the council – analogical similarity was.' Antinomies were replaced by analogies.[13]

It is true that Vatican II does not use the traditional terms such as *'primary and secondary analogates* and *intrinsic and extrinsic*

---

11 J. O'Malley, *What Happened at Vatican II* (Cambridge, MA: Harvard University Press, 2010).

12 Guarino, *Disputed Teaching*, p. 25.

13 Guarino, *Disputed Teaching*, pp. 73, 75.

attribution',[14] but analogical and participatory thinking under-girds whatever Vatican II says. The Church of Rome is never called the 'primary analogate' and the non-Catholic churches are never addressed as the 'secondary analogates'; yet it is clear that Vatican II stresses what is in common between the two because they are analogous to each other. The same is true as far as participatory categories are concerned. When Vatican II speaks of the modern world in friendly terms, wanting to affirm and to embrace it, it does so assuming that 'all human beings participate in the same created human nature, the ultimate ground of similarity among people'.[15] The notion of a 'diversified participation in a perfection'[16] undergirds modern Roman Catholic thought.

This is the theological background that allows Vatican II to talk about mutuality, friendship, partnership and cooperation with Protestants, Jews, Muslims, people of other religions, people of goodwill, the whole world. The council promotes a 'conciliatory approach – emphasizing unity with, rather than difference from, all others'.[17] Again, in Guarino's words, 'the "others" formally participate in the unique attributes of Catholicism and are therefore intensively related to it'.[18] This is not the fruit of a generic kindness, but the result of a particular theological project based on analogical and participatory categories. This does not mean that the traditional claims of Rome to be the only church, the perfect society and such like are obliterated. They are, however, no longer seen in exclusive and oppositional forms, but in analogous and participatory ways. It is no longer a matter of being 'in' or 'out', inside or outside, but it is a matter of participating at various degrees in the same reality. 'Without losing Catholic exceptionalism . . . the conciliar accent was placed on Catholicism's similarity' with other faiths.[19] They are now considered as 'partially similar to the Catholic faith and analogically

---

14 Guarino, *Disputed Teaching*, p. 27.
15 Guarino, *Disputed Teaching*, pp. 26–27.
16 Guarino, *Disputed Teaching*, p. 80.
17 Guarino, *Disputed Teaching*, p. 26.
18 Guarino, *Disputed Teaching*, p. 28.
19 Guarino, *Disputed Teaching*, p. 29.

related to it'.[20] Elsewhere Guarino argues that 'Catholicism did not change its self-understanding – but it did stress its close proximity to others'.[21] Vatican II presents the view whereby Rome has the fullness of grace, but those who do not belong to it still participate in it at various levels of intensity. According to Guarino, all this happened and is happening 'without betraying the material continuity of the faith' (i.e. the Roman Catholic faith).[22] We are back to the Catholic dynamics of 'development', 'ressourcement' and 'aggiornamento', that is, change without alteration, renewal without reformation, addition without purification.

Not away from Thomism but deeper into it

In pointing to the importance of this 'paradigm change'[23] in the present-day Roman Catholic Church, Guarino stands on the shoulders of giants of twentieth-century Catholic theology such as Gérard Philips, Karl Rahner, Yves Congar and Joseph Ratzinger.[24] His is not an isolated, fancy interpretation of Vatican II, but the mainstream reading of the theological principles at work in the Roman Catholic Church since the previous council.

Following Congar, Guarino further argues that the real theological mind behind Vatican II is not a modern theologian but Thomas Aquinas himself. It was Aquinas who 'furnished the writers of the dogmatic texts of Vatican II with the bases and structure (*les assises et la structure*) of their thought'.[25] Thomas's doctrine of analogy and his reinterpretation of the Neoplatonic doctrine of participation form the foundational axes of the theology of Vatican II. While the council avoided 'the *language* of scholasticism' it did make use of seminal 'scholastic *ideas*';[26] again, 'while Thomistic *language* was absent at Vatican II, Thomist *ideas* were in plain sight'.[27] While Vatican II practised an eclectic type of

20 Guarino, *Disputed Teaching*, p. 201.
21 Guarino, *Disputed Teaching*, p. 131.
22 Guarino, *Disputed Teaching*, p. 44.
23 Guarino, *Disputed Teaching*, p. 31.
24 Guarino, *Disputed Teaching*, pp. 30–31.
25 Guarino, *Disputed Teaching*, pp. 25, 74, 200.
26 Guarino, *Disputed Teaching*, p. 74; italics original.
27 Guarino, *Disputed Teaching*, p. 201; italics original.

'ressourcement', it was Thomas Aquinas who was the main source behind it. A modernized form of Thomism, perhaps a step away from the rigidity of nineteenth-century neo-Thomism but always within the same tradition expanded in the dialogue with the modern world, was and is the framework that provides 'the bases and structure' of Rome that will be seen in the next section on the 'problem' of Catholicism.

Three provisional implications

For evangelicals, what are the implications of such 'paradigm changes' that occurred at Vatican II? They are massive! Here are three tentative implications.

1. For the time being, Rome will not have an 'oppositional' posture in relating to non-Catholics but will always try to find common-alities, to underline unity, to stress fellowship and to embrace evangelicals as much as possible. Evangelicals need to be aware that if they want to be faithful to the gospel they need to be 'counter-cultural' and talk about gospel distinctives, biblical separation, and a covenantal allegiance to the triune God that rejects idols and idolatry. Biblical truth always needs to confront and to refute error even if it comes from a traditional institution like the Roman Catholic Church.

2. Even after Vatican II, Rome is not committed to the biblical gospel but is dedicated to the all-embracing gospel of 'analogy' and 'participation' that has translated into Rome's ecumenism, Mariology, ecclesiology, interreligious dialogue, mission and so on. Pope Francis may not even use the language of 'analogy' and 'participation', but his message of 'unity' and 'mercy' is steeped in it. Evangelicals need to become more acquainted with the basic motives of present-day Roman Catholicism if they want to grasp where Rome stands. The words used may be the same ('gospel', 'grace', 'faith', 'conversion', etc.), but their meaning is different because Rome uses them within the theological framework of Thomistic 'analogy' and 'participation'.

3. When Rome changes, it does so according to its own pattern of change. This change implies degrees of renewal that are always in the context of substantial continuity with its well-established self-understanding. Evangelicals need to learn to understand the Roman Catholic dynamics of change if they want to account for both continuity and discontinuity in present-day Rome. The Catholic Church may even talk about the need for a 'reformation', but this will always be below the standards of biblical reformation and always implemented in a way that self-protects the institution.

The problem of Roman Catholicism

Vatican II brought significant changes to the theological landscape of Roman Catholicism. Catholic theology found itself pushed towards a season of 'aggiornamento' (update). The retrieval of patristic influences introduced by the *nouvelle théologie* softened the rigidity of neo-Thomism as the main theological grid and nuanced many clear-cut boundaries that were prevalent before. Modern biblical criticism was introduced into biblical studies, thus blurring Rome's previous commitment to a high view of biblical inspiration. After Vatican II, there has been practically no distinction between critical scholarship done by Roman Catholic exegetes and that done by liberal Protestants in their study of Scripture. More broadly, after Vatican II, Roman Catholic theology connected with many modern trends like evolutionism, political theories, existentialism, feminism and religious studies, all developed in a highly sophisticated 'sacramental' way that is typical of Rome. Post-Vatican II Roman Catholic theology has become more 'catholic' and diverse in the sense of being more open to anything, embracing all trends and hospitable to all kinds of tendencies without losing its Roman institutional outlook. 'Dialogue' seems to be its catchword: dialogue with religions, dialogue with other Christian traditions, dialogue with the sciences, dialogue with social trajectories, dialogue with the secular world . . . Dialogue means expanding the boundaries, stretching the borders, rounding the edges, but not changing or moving the doctrinal core or the institutional centre of Rome.

Roman Catholicism is nuanced, diverse and yet a single world. A further question needs to be asked: what defines it? Is there something that qualifies not only parts of it but the whole of what Roman Catholicism stands for? Is there a core element that shapes all components in a distinct way and links its words to a coherent vision? On this question, scores of heavyweight theologians have written masterful analyses over the centuries and up to this day. From John Henry Newman to Romano Guardini, from Johann Adam Möhler to Karl Adam, from Hans Urs von Balthasar to Henri de Lubac, from Avery Dulles to Walter Kasper, dozens of authors have tried to identify what makes Roman Catholicism what it is. Despite the different suggestions provided, the common assumption is that Roman Catholicism is an interconnected whole and that its identity is pervasively present – though with different intensities – in all its expressions.

The latest attempt to identify the theological DNA of Catholicism comes from the pen of Karl-Heinz Menke, professor of theology at the University of Bonn and one of the most authoritative voices of present-day Roman Catholic theology in Germany. His book *Sakramentalität: Wesen und Wunde des Katholizismus* (2015) (English: *Sacramentality: The essence and the wounds of Catholicism*) exactly tackles this issue and is a useful new contribution to the whole discussion.[28] A full review of the book is beyond the scope of this section, but at least two points are worth exploring.

Roman Catholicism as a whole

Menke speaks of the essence of Roman Catholicism in terms of its 'thought form' and 'life form'. Quoting Greshake,[29] he agrees with his approach:

The Christian faith is not a jumble of single truths: here a dogma, there a dogma, here an exegetical point, there a moral

---

28 I had access to the Italian translation: Karl-Heinz Menke, *Sacramentalità: essenza e ferite del cattolicesimo* (Brescia: Queriniana, 2015). Quotations will be taken and referenced from this volume; translations from the Italian into English are my own.

29 G. Greshake, 'Was trennt? Überlegungen zur konfessionellen Grunddifferenz', *Theologie der Gegenwart* 49 (2006), pp. 162–174, quotation from p. 162s.

norm, etc. Faith is rather a structured and coherent whole. This has important consequences for the interconfessional theological dialogue: in the end it is of little use to talk from time to time (only) about individual topics and to seek consensus about them; rather one must ask: what is the ultimate reason for the different view of this or of that single theme? If we proceed in this way, we will come across an ultimate diversity in the overall conception of revelation, a diversity that is concretized in the various individual categorical differences. This means that among the individual confessions, in the final analysis there are no differences but there is a fundamental difference which then unfolds in a series of differences.[30]

Since the context of this argument deals with the differences between Roman Catholicism and the Protestant faith (although he has primarily in mind liberal Protestantism), there are several points to be highlighted here:

1 faith is a 'structured and coherent whole';
2 the dialogue between evangelicals and Catholics must seek to identify the ultimate motif of the respective faiths and conduct it accordingly;
3 this ultimate motif is apparent in all expressions of theology and practice;
4 the difference between confessions (i.e. Roman Catholicism and Protestantism) is traceable to a 'fundamental difference' that unfolds in a 'series of differences'.

It is important that Roman Catholic theologians of this calibre suggest such a clear view of what is at stake. Often, people who are involved in ecumenical dialogue show little awareness of the 'systemic' (my word, not Menke's) nature of their own faith and the other group's faith. The popular version of this superficial approach is seen when it is argued that as far as evangelicals and Catholics are

---

30 Menke, *Sacramentalità*, p. 12.

concerned, 'we agree on Christology, but we disagree on soteriology and ecclesiology', or 'we agree on the Trinity, but we disagree on Mary', as if theology were made up of a bunch of isolated elements. If we follow Menke and Greshake, it is not theologically feasible to hold such an 'atomistic' approach (again, my term, not Menke's), as if doctrines were disconnected bits and pieces. On the contrary, the Roman Catholic views of salvation, the church and Mary are shaped around Roman Catholic accounts of the Trinity and Christ. Doctrines and practices cannot be disjoined as if they existed in independent silos. Rather, they must be seen as mutually influencing one another. In other words, Roman Catholicism is a coherent and unified whole, and therefore must be seen as stemming from the 'overall conception of revelation' that leads to an 'ultimate diversity' with regard to the evangelical faith.

Sacramentality as the essence

Given the theologically unified and coherent nature of Roman Catholicism, what is its essence then? According to the Bonn theologian, the essence lies in the 'thought form' (*Denkform*) that is shaped by sacramentality: 'the Catholic thought form and life form is essentially sacramental'.[31] Again, 'the sacramental thought form of Catholicism is the difference that contributes to explaining all the rest'.[32]

There are three sides to Menke's understanding of sacramentality:

1 the sacramental representation of the church of Jesus Christ in space and time;
2 the sacramental actualization of the humanity of Jesus Christ through the liturgy, ministry and dogma of the church as an institution visibly united in the successors of the apostles;
3 the sacramental presence of the absolute in the story of Jesus (original sacrament) and his church (fundamental sacrament).[33]

---

31 Menke, *Sacramentalità*, p. 14.
32 Menke, *Sacramentalità*, p. 27.
33 Menke, *Sacramentalità*, p. 40.

There is a whole theological universe here that would need a lot of unpacking. Simply put, the essence of Roman Catholicism is its view of the relationship between Christ and church in terms of sacramental representation; the relationship between the humanity of Christ and the institutional and hierarchical church in terms of sacramental actualization of the former in the latter; and the relationship between Christ and whatever the church is and does in terms of sacramental presence. The sacramentality of the church is the mode of Christ's presence in the world in and through the Roman Catholic Church. We will try to further unpack what sacramentality means in terms of the Christ–church relationship.

The point is that Roman Catholicism has its core in the interconnection between Christ and the church, between Christology and ecclesiology. Everything else stems from this 'essence' that makes Christ and the church coinherent and their relationship sacramental. The sacramentality of the Roman Church does not entail the seven sacraments only, but the whole of the church in its self-understanding, life and practices.

Sacramentality refers to the idea of 'mediation': since nature is intrinsically capable of being elevated by grace, grace is not received immediately or externally but always through a vehicle or a natural vector. The sacrament is the natural 'lever' with which divine grace is communicated to nature. From the Roman Catholic sacramental point of view, the grace of baptism is imparted with water, that of extreme unction with oil, that of ordination with the imposition of hands, that of the Eucharist with consecrated bread and wine. Grace cannot be received 'by faith alone' but always through a natural element imparted by the church, which acts in the name of Christ and transforms it from a merely natural element to the 'real presence' of divine grace.

There are therefore two elements necessary for the Roman Catholic sacrament: a physical–natural element and the agency of the church, which is believed to have the task of transfiguring matter and imparting grace. Therefore, the natural object becomes grace and the church is in charge of administering it. The interdependence between nature and grace means that grace comes into nature and through nature; the interconnection between Christ and the church makes the Church of Rome dispense it in the name of Christ himself. Since it is Christ who works through the sacraments of the church, these have an effect *ex opere operato* (by the very fact of being imparted).

In response to the Protestant Reformation, which had emphasized that the work of Christ is received by faith alone through the work of the Holy Spirit, the Council of Trent (1545–63) designed the sacramental layout of the Church of Rome: from baptism to extreme unction, a sacramental journey is envisaged for the Catholic faithful. The journey is made up of seven sacraments (baptism, confirmation, confession, the Eucharist, ordination, marriage, extreme unction) that accompany a human being from birth to death. The Roman Church dispenses God's grace in every age and throughout life. Some sacraments are administrations of grace received once and for all (i.e. baptism, confirmation, ordination, marriage, extreme unction); others are received cyclically and repeatedly (confession and the Eucharist). In this way, God's grace becomes 'real' and pervasive through the action of the church. For the Council of Trent, being excluded from the sacraments (by excommunication, schism or belonging to other religions) was equivalent to being excluded from grace.

While not denying the Tridentine system, the Second Vatican Council (1962–5) added an important emphasis. The last council shifted attention from the sacramental acts of the Catholic Church to the sacramental essence of the church. In the famous conciliar definition, 'the Church is in Christ like a sacrament or as a sign and instrument both of a very closely knit union with God and of the unity of the whole human race' (*LG* 1). It is the church as such that is a sacrament, that is, the 'real presence' of Christ. It is so as a 'sign and instrument': an already given reality and also an agent at the service of its growth. The church expresses unity with God and the unity of the whole human race. The Roman Catholic Church is thought of as a sign and instrument of the unity of all women and men. For this reason, Rome can speak of everyone as 'brothers and sisters': those whom Trent considered excluded from grace because they were excluded from the sacraments (Protestants, Muslims, Jews, etc.), the Church of Rome now considers as 'brothers and sisters' already touched by grace (albeit in a mysterious way) and already in some way ordained to the Catholic Church. From the sacraments as specific acts, to the sacramentality of the church as a whole: this is where the Roman Catholic Church stands today.

The gospel recognizes the goodness of creation but also the radical nature of sin. Human beings by their nature do not receive the things of the Spirit if these are not revealed to them (1 Cor. 2:12–15). The flesh (the sinful nature) does not receive grace: it is the Spirit who gives life (John 6:63). Jesus instituted the ordinances of baptism and the Lord's Supper as 'visible words' (according to the beautiful expression of the Italian Reformer Peter Martyr Vermigli) that testify to the grace received by faith, not as objects through which grace is made present by a church that believes itself to be the extension of the incarnation of Jesus Christ.

There are, therefore, far-reaching consequences for an evangelical assessment of Roman Catholicism. Among other things, this means that the 'essence' of Roman Catholicism is its account of Christology, and therefore the Trinity, and the way in which it shapes the broad reality of the church. This is not a secondary issue. It lies at the heart of the faith: the Roman Catholic account of the person, the work and the doctrine of Christ. The problem of Roman Catholicism does not primarily lie in its Mariology, in its unbiblical folk devotions or in papal infallibility. These, and many others, are all variations that arise from the ultimate difference, which has to do with the account of Jesus Christ himself and his relationship with the church.

According to Menke, Protestantism is a 'wound' of the faith. In his view, the evangelical insistence on Scripture alone, faith alone and glory to God alone are ways in which the Roman sacramental link is severed. There is an element of truth in this analysis. According to the evangelical account of the gospel, Christ stands above the church through Scripture exercising his authority over his people; Christ stands above the church in having accomplished the work of salvation and granting its benefits to believers; Christ stands above the church by leading the church to the worship of the triune God away from idolatry. The essence of Roman Catholicism is ultimately different from the essence of the evangelical faith.

The two axes of Roman Catholicism

The language used by Menke is that of sacramentality. For the time being, it is important to notice that Roman Catholicism is not a set of theological words and religious practices randomly related. A global view of Roman Catholicism must take into account its doctrine, practices and institutions. It is a religious world view which has been promoted throughout history by the ecclesiastical institution whose centre is in Rome. Although there is considerable diversity in its forms of expression, Roman Catholicism is basically a unitary reality whose underlying tenets can be discerned. Any analysis which does not take into account the fact that Roman Catholicism is a system will fall prey to a superficial and fragmented understanding of it. It is an all-encompassing 'world' that stands on two axes.

1. Roman Catholicism's starting point has to be located in the relationship between 'nature' and 'grace' into which is engrafted the idea of the church as the extension of the incarnation of the Son of God. Both of these themes can be presented with subtle diversity and with any number of interpretative variations, but by virtue of the fact that they form Roman Catholicism's theological framework, they will always be present. This basic orientation in its presuppositions explains why Roman Catholicism has little sense of the tragedy of sin, tends to encourage an optimistic view of human abilities, sees salvation as a process in which nature is made more perfect, and justifies the church's role as a mediator between human beings and God.

In Roman Catholicism there are two main axes that form its *framework*: on the one hand, as Gregg Allison has helpfully named it, the 'nature–grace interdependence' and, on the other, the 'Christ–church interconnection'.[34] Historically, the Roman magisterium has

---

34 I borrow these expressions from G. R. Allison, *Roman Catholic Theology and Practice: An evangelical assessment* (Wheaton, IL: Crossway, 2014), pp. 42–67.

given assent to both the Augustinian tradition (philosophically influenced by Neoplatonic thought) and the Thomistic tradition (emerging from a Christian reinterpretation of Aristotle via Aquinas). Whereas Augustinianism has stressed the corrupting reality of sin and the utter primacy of grace, Thomism has given a more positive account of human nature's intrinsic disposition towards the operations of grace. Both traditions manage to coexist, in that the Roman Catholic system provides a sufficiently capable platform which can host both while not being totally identified or identifiable with any one of them. This is another significant pointer to the catholicity of the system itself.

The spheres of nature and grace are thus in irreversible theological continuity, as 'nature' in Roman Catholicism incorporates both creation and sin, in contrast to the Reformed distinction between creation, sin and redemption. This differing understanding of sin's impact means grace finds in nature a receptive attitude (enabling Roman Catholicism's humanistic optimism), as against a biblical doctrine whereby entrenched sin leaves us unaware of our reprobate state. Nature is seen as 'open' to grace. Although nature has been touched by sin, it is still programmatically open to be infused, elevated, supplemented by grace. The Roman Catholic 'mild' view of the fall and of sin makes it possible for Rome to hold a view of nature that is tainted by sin but not depraved, obscured but not blinded, wounded but not alienated, morally disordered but not spiritually dead, inclined to evil but still holding on to what is true, good and beautiful.[35] There is always a residual good in nature that grace can and must work with. After Vatican II, more recent interpretations of the nature–grace interdependence go so far as arguing that nature is always graced from within.[36] If traditional Roman Catholicism maintained that grace was *added* to nature, present-day Rome prefers to talk about grace as being an *infrastructure* of nature. In spite of the differences between the two versions, the interdependence is nonetheless underlined.

---

35 The Roman Catholic teaching on sin can be found in *CCC* 1849–1875.
36 S. Duffy, *The Graced Horizon: Nature and grace in modern Catholic thought* (Collegeville, MN: Liturgical Press, 1992).

The nature–grace interdependence, in all its various forms and degrees, is the reason why Roman Catholicism nurtures an optimism in the ability of human beings to know and to follow God's will and to cooperate with his grace. It also explains the idea whereby the physical world can transmit the grace of God – even becoming the body of Christ (as happens with the consecrated species of the Eucharist). Finally, it helps explain the ability of Roman Catholicism to embrace and integrate (often falling into syncretism) all cultures, all religions, the whole of humanity into its liturgies, practices and devotions. This interdependence underpins Rome's hyper-veneration of Mary. Mary is the embodiment of *natura pura* (pure nature), immaculate with regard to original sin, and the idealized projection of every human being. The Roman Catholic epistemological openness, its trust in human abilities and its overall reliance on the possibility of human cooperation all converge in the Roman Catholic account of Mary. She is the quintessential expression of the Roman Catholic view of the relationship between nature and grace.

2. Roman Catholicism needs a mediating subject to relate grace to nature and nature to grace – namely, the Roman Church – and thus Allison speaks of the 'Christ–church interconnection'. The church is considered a prolongation of the incarnation, mirroring Christ as a divine–human reality, acting as an *altera persona Christi*, a second 'Christ'. It is therefore impossible for Roman Catholics to cry with the Reformers 'Solus Christus!', for this would be seen as breaching the organic bond between Christ and the church. The threefold ministry of Christ as King, Priest and Prophet is thus transposed to the Roman Church – in its hierarchical rule, its magisterial interpretation of the Word and its administration of the sacraments. There is never *solus Christus* (Christ alone), only *Christus in ecclesia* (Christ in the church) and *ecclesia in Christo* (the church in Christ).

If Jesus Christ is true man and true God (as affirmed at the Council of Nicaea, AD 325), the church, by virtue of a 'not weak analogy' (*LG* 8), is 'one complex reality which coalesces from a divine and a human element' (idem). In the words of the encyclical *Mystici Corporis Christi* (The Mystical Body of Christ) of Pius XII (1943) the church subsists 'almost like a second person of Christ'. Thus, the ecclesial self-understanding of Roman Catholicism is based on a Christological point. As Jesus Christ is true man and true God, so the church is a *theandric* (divine and human) organism united to Christ and one with him. This wrong view of the relationship has enormous consequences for the whole of theology and practice.

The emphasis on the Christ–church interconnection seems to forget that the church is still a divine creature, belonging to the reality created by God and marked by sin, while Christ is the divine Creator, the One from whom all things are and who is perfect now and always. When we talk about Christology, we are talking about the unique relationship between human nature and divine nature in the person of Jesus Christ on the side of the Creator; when we talk about ecclesiology, we are talking about the unity of divine and human elements from the side of creation. The distinction between Creator and creature is decisive for not falling into the trap of elevating the church into a quasi-divine body.

Blurred times and distinctions

As Gregg Allison has usefully named it, the Christ–church inter-connection is the second axis that is based on a blurred view of the relationship between Christ and the church.[37] In an important book, John Stott proposed the idea that the message of the gospel may be summed up adequately by two biblical adverbs which are linked to the concept of time: *hapax* (once and for all) and *mallon* (for evermore).[38] It is around these two words that both the uniqueness and the definitive character of the incarnation are asserted, and the dynamic, progressive nature of the sanctifying action of the Holy Spirit articulated. The terms refer to two important aspects of the work of the trinitarian God in the world. The first (*hapax*) is circumscribed by time and is definitive in regard to the completion of the work of salvation. The other (*mallon*) proceeds throughout time

---

37 In what follows, I condense the argument made in my article 'The blurring of time distinctions in Roman Catholicism', *Themelios* 29.2 (2004), pp. 40–46.
38 J. Stott, *Evangelical Truth: A personal plea for unity* (Leicester: Inter-Varsity Press, 1999).

and develops the outworking of salvation in history. The gospel is a message that is based on what God has done (*hapax*) and on what he is doing (*mallon*). The demarcation that differentiates the two terms may be subtle, but it must be maintained in order to avoid any distortion of the fundamental structure of the Christian faith. Even the tiniest of violations could become devastating, producing effects of enormous consequence.

The argument suggested here is that Roman Catholicism performs a crucial breach of the boundary between *hapax* and *mallon* with its understanding of the church as a prolongation of the incarnation. This breach subsequently caused a series of further incursions that affect the whole of the Roman Catholic theological fabric.

Confusing *hapax* and *mallon*

Roman Catholic ecclesiology is built on the idea of the continuation of the incarnation of the Son of God in his mystical body, that is, the church. Adam Möhler's classic definition is helpful here: 'The visible Church . . . is the Son of God himself, everlastingly manifesting himself among men in a human form, perpetually renovated, and eternally young – the permanent incarnation of the same.'[39] This 'incarnational' understanding of the church, rooted in the Counter-Reformation tradition and renewed in recent authoritative teaching[40] and theological reflection,[41] is the key to understanding the basic framework of Roman Catholic ecclesiology.

However, it must be remembered that the incarnation of Christ is a *hapax* (once-and-for-all event) in the work of God which is

---

39 J. A. Möhler, *Symbolism or Exposition of the Doctrinal Differences between Catholics and Protestants as Evidenced by Their Symbolic Writings* (London: Gibbings & Co., 1906), p. 259.
40 E.g. *LG* 8, 10–12; *CCC* 737, 766, 787–788, 795.
41 According to Yves Congar, 'the idea that sees in the church the continuation of the Incarnation has been long recurring in catholic theology (St. Thomas Aquinas, S. Francis of Sales, Bousset, Fénelon, etc.)': Y. Congar, 'Dogme christologique et ecclésiologie: verité et limites d'un parallèle', in A. Grillmeier and H. Bacht, *Das Konzil von Chalkedon: Geschichte und Gegenwart*, vol. 3, 2nd edn (Würzburg: Echter Verlag, 1959), pp. 239–268; the quotation is on p. 239. The same essay by Congar can be found in his *Sainte Église: études et approches ecclésiologiques* (Paris: Cerf, 1963), pp. 53–104. On the more modern expressions of the same view, see R. Baglioni, *La chiesa 'continua incarnazione' del Verbo: da J. A. Möhler al Concilio Vaticano II* (Naples: Editrice Domenicana Italiana, 2013).

uniquely related to the person and mission of the Son so that it neither requires any supplement or continuation, nor any integration or representation. The very fact that Christ is seated at the right hand of the Father is the supreme culmination of his earthly mission. It is done. In Roman Catholic thought, however, while the virgin birth is rightly considered to be the beginning of the incarnation, the ascension does not represent a definitive end of Christ's work in salvation which confirms its uniqueness and completeness. Instead it is considered as part of a process which, although changing the mode of Christ's presence (from a physical to a mystical presence), carries out the continuation of his incarnation in the nature and mission of the church. A substantial continuity remains between the incarnation of the Son and the work of the church, and that carries with it serious consequences.

The act of having blurred the unique and definitive nature of the incarnation with its glorious conclusion at the ascension implies the transferral of the mission of the Son from Christ to the church. By overthrowing the *hapax* (once and for all) of the incarnation in favour of its continuation through the church, Christ's prerogatives are aligned with those of the church.[42] The unique mediation of Christ yields to the mediation of the church. The regal authority of Christ is absorbed into the jurisdictional power of the church. The final revelation of Christ is subsequently administered by the magisterial office of the church and, given that it also embraces oral tradition, at times results in the emergence of other truths that are not attested in biblical revelation. The choice of the apostles by Christ, instead of being a once-and-for-all event, evolves into the succession of bishops, which is established by the ecclesiastical institution. The prerogatives of salvation that belong solely to Christ are indirectly (but really) attributed to Mary, who shares with the Son an assumption into heaven. The worship that is attributed exclusively to God is also deflected to other figures, even if this is only in the

---

42 On the transposition of the threefold office of Christ (king, prophet and priest) to the Roman Church, cf. the stimulating critique by V. Subilia, *The Problem of Catholicism*, tr. R. Kissack (Philadelphia, PA: Westminster Press, 1964). On the same subject, cf. also M. Saucy's 'Evangelicals, Catholics, and Orthodox together: is the church the extension of the incarnation?', *Journal of the Evangelical Theological Society* 43.2 (2000), pp. 193–212.

form of veneration. In short, the *hapax* of Christ continues in the *mallon* of the church. The time period of Christ becomes identified with, and actualized in, the time of the church, just as the time of the church is always thought of as a direct continuation of the time of Christ. The *hapax* sense of biblical revelation is opened up to being integrated with the *mallon* of tradition of the church that is mediated by the magisterium, thus creating a theology of the Word that is greater than the Bible and an authority structure that goes beyond the Word of God written.

The sacrifice of Christ is represented in the sacrament of the church (i.e. the Eucharist) that makes it present. Because the church is involved in the time of the incarnation of the Son, it is also active in his redemption which is accomplished on the cross. Both the incarnation and redemption are understood as *mallon* (for evermore) instead of *hapax* (once and for all). The *Catechism of the Catholic Church* affirms the uniqueness (614, 618) and perfection (529) of Christ's sacrifice at Calvary. The uniqueness of salvation history intersects, however, with the eucharistic developments in such a way that what is affirmed about the sacrifice of Christ becomes integrated with the language of re-presentation (1366), perpetuation (611, 1323) and making present (1362). The Eucharist is the sacrifice of Christ re-enacted, perpetuated and made present. Among other things, this means that as the cross is a sacrifice, so too the Eucharist is a sacrifice (1330, 1365), to the point where together they are 'one single sacrifice' (1367). The uniqueness of the cross is explained in loose terms in order to include the Eucharist so that the *hapax* of Calvary is dissolved into the *mallon* of the Mass. The work of the cross, therefore, is considered definitive but not final. Above all, it is unable to actualize its own efficacy without the active participation of the church in making it present. Given the fact that the enactment of the Eucharist is a supplement necessary in making the cross effective, it is in the Mass that the real work of redemption is carried out (1364).[43]

---

43 See the previous discussion in ch. 2 on the relationship between the cross, the church and the Eucharist.

The same theological rationale can be seen in the doctrine of papal infallibility (elevated to dogma in 1870) which ascribes to the pope the divine prerogative of infallibility. Here too this doctrine is based on the conviction that the divine infallibility of Jesus Christ is communicated to the leadership of the church which prolongs the incarnation. In this understanding of the church as a 'continuous incarnation' of the Word, what can be said of the infallibility of Jesus Christ can also be predicated of the church, his body which extends his presence in the world.

The Protestant Reformation identified the core of the problem with Roman Catholicism in its mingling of what ought to remain distinct. *Solus Christus* and *sola scriptura* are none other than an urgent call to rigorously respect the *hapax* of the gospel in order to benefit from it more and more. In fact, enjoying the *mallon* of the gospel is only possible after respecting its *hapax*. Looking at Roman Catholicism today, it is hard to believe that that call has been superseded. Therefore, the Protestant teaching of *solus Christus* (Christ alone) is the vindication of the fundamental distinction between the Creator and the creature. The integrity of the *hapax* of the incarnation is a safeguard against any attempt to infringe the uniqueness of God and to allow others to 'participate' in what belongs to him and to him alone.

Misleading view of *totus Christus*

The blurring of what is proper to God and what is proper to his creatures has another facet that goes back to a faulty interpretation of the Church Father Augustine (AD 354–430) as he understands the relationship between Christ and the church. One of the most controversial points of his theology is his conception of the *totus Christus*, the 'total Christ': the idea that the unity of Christ with the church is so deep as to form a single mystery.[44] The Head of the body is so united with the body of the Head to become a single Christ. On this doctrine, Roman Catholicism built its own theology of the

---

44 Here I rely on this collection of Augustine's texts on the topic: Sant'Agostino, *Il Cristo totale*, ed. G. Carrabetta (Rome: Città Nuova, 2012); translations from the Italian into English are my own.

prolongation of the incarnation in the church. It is as if there were such an intrinsic and profound union between Christ and the church as to make it possible, indeed necessary, to see the church as the sacramental extension of the incarnation of the Son of God. In fact, there are texts in which Augustine throws himself into peremptory statements in which, speaking of the church united to Christ, he affirms that 'we are Christ' (*Enarrationes in Psalmos* 26/2, 2; *Sermones* 144.5) or 'we have become Christ' (*In Iohannis Evangelium Tractatus* 21,8). The whole Christ 'is head and body' (*Enarrationes in Psalmos* 30/2, 3). At best, these would be ambiguous expressions if they had not been accompanied and supplemented by an orthodox Christology like that of Augustine. Besides the blurred statements about the *totus Christus*, Augustine, speaking of Christ, writes that 'even without us, he is complete' (*Sermones* 341, 9.11). Christ does not need the ecclesial body to be Christ. Elsewhere Augustine writes: 'He is the Creator, we are the creatures; he is the craftsman, we are the work made by him, he the moulder, we the moulded ones' (*Sermones* 91, 7.8). His doctrine of the total Christ, however ambiguous and confused it is, does not break the distinction between Creator and creature and does not elevate the church (the body) to the status of divinity.

Having said that, Augustine's interpretation of Colossians 1:24, Acts 9:4 and Ephesians 5 on the relationship between Christ and the church in a spousal perspective led him to affirm the organic nature of that relationship and to go so far as affirming the 'totality' of their being combined. The comments on the same texts also indicate the problematic direction of his theology on the 'deification' of the Christian, that is, his or her incorporation into the person of Christ, becoming part of the mystical body.[45] Indeed, one can understand how Roman Catholicism was dazzled by the metaphor of the total Christ, going far beyond Augustine and developing it in the theology of the Eucharist (the 'real presence' of Christ), of the priesthood (the priest acting *in altera persona Christi* [in the person of Christ]) and the development of dogma (the Roman Church being endowed with

---

45 On this point see D. V. Meconi, *The One Christ: St. Augustine's theology of deification* (Lanham, MD: Catholic University of America Press, 2013).

the authority of Christ in promulgating dogmas). The Augustinian interpretation on this point is therefore subject to different uses, depending on what one wants to see in his texts as the primary element: the blurred *totus Christus* or the preserved distinction between Creator and creature.

Rome interprets the Augustinian reference to *totus Christus* as a union which blurs the distinction between the Head and the body. The *Catechism* teaches that 'Christ and his Church thus together make up the "whole Christ" (*Christus totus*). The church is one with Christ' (795). According to Subilia, in this mistake lies the 'problem of Catholicism'.[46] In this unsurpassed study, Subilia deals with the reason why the Church of Rome has such a high and excessive view of itself and is inclined to claim divine prerogatives. Subilia touches precisely on the ecclesiology of Augustine, one of whose essential components can be summarized in the expression *totus Christus*. According to Augustine, there is a relationship between Christ and the church so organic and profound that the church becomes part of the whole Christ. Subilia notes that Augustine, who had been a Manichean, therefore a dualist, suffered the opposite temptation of 'monism' (i.e. the reduction to one) in his thought. While emphasizing the distinction between the Head and the members and therefore between Christ and the church, in Augustine 'the sovereignty of the Head over the body is disastrously lost to view'.[47] The expressions 'one flesh' and 'one body' used in the Bible to denote the relationship between husband and wife are used to describe the relationship between Christ and the church. Augustine transposes the relational unity reflecting the unity of a married couple to an ontological principle qualifying the Christ–church interconnection. Defending Augustine and the Roman Catholic interpretation of the Church Father, Gherardini summarizes the ecclesiology of the *totus Christus* as 'Christ continued and identified in the Church'.[48]

---

46 V. Subilia, *The Problem of Catholicism* (Philadelphia, PA: Westminster Press, 1964).
47 Subilia, *Problem of Catholicism*, p. 116.
48 B. Gherardini, *La cattolica: lineamenti d'ecclesiologia agostiniana* (Turin: Lindau, 2011), p. 29.

Starting from Augustine, Roman Catholic ecclesiology became radicalized in emphasizing the theme of the unity between Christ and the church in terms of a hierarchical–sacramental church representing Christ on earth. For Subilia, this is a 'damage so deep-seated that the very life-centres of the Christian organism are affected, and it is being changed into quite a different organism'.[49] If this reading is plausible, the 'problem of Catholicism' is not merely in one doctrine or in some superficial differences on secondary issues. Its problem lies at the very heart of its system and is pervasively present in all its expressions: from the Trinity to Mariology, from the sacraments to soteriology, from ecclesiology to the manifold devotions. Everything is infected by it.

The ultimate issue:
Yes and No to the gospel

As was shown above, there is something deep that runs through Roman Catholic doctrine and practice that makes it different from the biblical gospel. No matter which doctrine or practice you observe, there is always something that departs from Scripture and ends up far away from it, while still using its words. The degree and intensity of the departure is not always the same, but it is always there. Why? What is so intrinsic to Roman Catholicism that causes it to deviate from the gospel? There is a biblical passage that can help in coming to terms with what happens in Roman Catholicism all the time and at all points. The apostle Paul in 2 Corinthians 1:15–22 points out to the church the need to be always committed to the Yes of the gospel and to refuse to blur it with marred answers made up of both Yes and No.[50] Here is the text:

> [15]Because I was sure of this, I wanted to come to you first, so that you might have a second experience of grace. [16]I wanted to visit you on my way to Macedonia, and to come back to you

---

49 Subilia, *Problem of Catholicism*, p. 119.
50 It is always rewarding to read the commentary on this passage by C. Hodge, *Second Epistle to the Corinthians: An exposition* (London: The Banner of Truth Trust, 1959), pp. 21–26.

from Macedonia and have you send me on my way to Judea. [17]Was I vacillating when I wanted to do this? Do I make my plans according to the flesh, ready to say 'Yes, yes' and 'No, no' at the same time? [18]As surely as God is faithful, our word to you has not been Yes and No. [19]For the Son of God, Jesus Christ, whom we proclaimed among you, Silvanus and Timothy and I, was not Yes and No, but in him it is always Yes. [20]For all the promises of God find their Yes in him. That is why it is through him that we utter our Amen to God for his glory. [21]And it is God who establishes us with you in Christ, and has anointed us, [22]and who has also put his seal on us and given us his Spirit in our hearts as a guarantee.

The context of the passage could be thus summarized: in the course of performing Paul's service, there was a change in the plans for the apostolic itinerary. The reasons for this change will be explained later on in the letter (see 2 Cor. 1:23 – 2:4), but we do know that the change had caused some perplexity within the church of Corinth. In this passage Paul confronts the criticisms that had been addressed to him concerning his alleged superficial attitude in planning his journey.

Now, the questions of the changes in his itinerary are the opportunity which Paul uses to deal with a more profound issue. Paul appears to be aware of the fact that criticisms were not raised simply to question his ability to plan his activities but had a much deeper intent: to undermine the very basis of the apostolic service, discredit Paul's preaching and disown his apostolic authority. What is at stake here is not so much the apostolic programme as the apostolic message, not so much the stages of Paul's journey as the preaching of Paul's gospel. The question is much more serious than that. To the accusations of instability and unreliability, Paul replies by going back to the distinctive traits of his gospel preaching: 'our word to you has not been Yes and No,' he says at verse 18. The message had not been ambiguous and contradictory as the accusations would lead us to believe. Later Paul takes a further step in vindicating the coherence of the gospel and its roots in God's promises, fulfilled by Christ. The message was coherent in that at verse 19 he says: 'For the Son of God,

Jesus Christ, whom we proclaimed among you . . . was not Yes and No, but in him it is always Yes.' What was preached was not a Yes and a No because Jesus Christ himself is the Yes of God's promises. In this way, the apostolic preaching was 'the Amen to God for his glory' (v. 20), the obedient Yes of faith to the Yes of the promises fulfilled by Jesus Christ.

Now, what does this passage tell us about Roman Catholicism? Borrowing the language of 2 Corinthians it is possible to argue that Roman Catholicism is the religion of the Yes and No to God's truth at the same time, of the assertion and denial of the biblical message, of the coexistence of submission to and rejection of God's Word. It cannot be denied that the Yes is present to some degree in Roman Catholicism (i.e. the words inherited by the church of the first centuries); the problem stems from the fact that it is not a 'Yes, yes' but that it is a Yes and No at the same time. The Yes is juxtaposed to the No so as to produce an invalidating effect on the Yes; it is not Yes, nor is it No, but it is Yes and No at the same time. How does this come about?

For example, Christ is told Yes but also No because, in the Catholic view, the prerogatives of the church end up by arrogating what belongs exclusively to Jesus Christ as Lord and Saviour. As to grace, it is told Yes but also No because, in line with Roman Catholicism, nature holds in itself the capacity to be elevated in spite of sin. Faith is told Yes but also No because, according to Rome, in order to receive God's grace there is the need for the sacramental instrumentality of the church, which makes faith insufficient. The Word of God is told Yes but also No inasmuch as the Scriptures are sidelined by the tradition of the Roman Catholic church and its teaching, which end up prevailing over the Bible. The church worship rendered to God is told Yes but also No because the hyper-veneration of Mary is encouraged, as well as the veneration of a host of other side figures, which detracts from the worship of the one and only God.

The evangelical faith is, on the contrary, the faith of a Yes which aspires to be a firm, convinced, unequivocal, exclusive response to God's truth; it is the 'Amen to God for his glory', the acknowledgment, the conformation of it. In this, it takes form and character because of its 'simplicity' and 'sincerity' (v. 12), because it flees from following 'earthly wisdom' (v. 12) and because is not nurtured 'according to the flesh' (v. 17), again to echo Paul's words in 2 Corinthians. The evangelical faith, as much as it concerns the foundations of the faith, chooses them on the basis of faithfulness and integrity according to the Scriptures, and, in continuity with the biblical message and the teaching of the Protestant Reformation, proclaims the renowned *solas*:

- *Christ alone.* The Christian faith hinges on the person, work and prerogatives of Jesus Christ. Salvation is entirely through him and leads to him alone.
- *Scripture alone.* The Bible is the supreme authority for the faith and for the whole of life: other authorities are subjected to the Bible.
- *Grace alone.* Salvation comes from the undeserved and unconditional favour of God and is not entrusted to the administration of the church, nor mediated by any priestly class.
- *Faith alone.* The means of receiving God's grace is faith, that is, the awareness of what Christ did, the sincere acceptance of his message and the placing of total trust in him.
- *To God alone be the glory.* Worship is to be rendered only and exclusively to the triune God, Lord of heaven and earth, to the Creator, Provider and Saviour of the world. All forms of devotion and veneration rendered to human beings must be rejected as having a tendency towards idolatry.

Here lies the whole difference between Roman Catholicism and the gospel. Roman Catholicism can be viewed as the haughty 'earthly wisdom', a majestic cathedral of human thought, a fascinating religiously ideological structure, ever expanding; the evangelical faith on the contrary aspires solely to remain a simple and sincere 'amen' to the Word of God. All the *solas* of the biblical message which the Reformers rediscovered bear witness to the integrity of the evangelical faith which refuses to be contaminated by pagan motivations, choosing instead to be exclusively anchored to God's truth and aimed at the worship of God alone. It simply upholds the Yes of God's truth which the gospel heralds.

In closing, there are perhaps no more adequate words than those elaborated by the World Evangelical Fellowship in its 1986 *Perspective on Roman Catholicism*. Chronologically, they were written prior to the publication of the *Catechism* and specifically refer to the Roman Catholic view of the sacraments, but nonetheless, they well apply to the thrust of present-day Roman Catholicism:

> At bottom, our evangelical critique of Roman Catholic sacramentology points up the conflict between two opposing views of the Christian faith. Rome sees itself as an extension of the incarnation, thus divinizing human beings as they cooperate with God's grace that is conferred by the church. Over against this view stands our evangelical commitment to the free gift of righteousness, imputed solely by the grace of God, received by a true faith that answers to God's Word, and based fully upon the once-for-all expiation of guilt through the finished sacrifice of the perfect Substitute, Christ Jesus. This confession is for us the gospel.[51]

Each biblical 'word' contained in this quotation ('faith', 'grace', 'church', 'righteousness', 'God's Word', 'expiation', 'sacrifice', 'confession') is endorsed by Rome, but the Roman Catholic 'world' shapes it in such a way that it does not lead to the same confession of the gospel. The problem is in the flawed system of Roman Catholicism that results in an opposing view of the Christian faith.

---

51 P. G. Schrotenboer (ed.), *Roman Catholicism: A contemporary evangelical perspective* (Grand Rapids, MI: Baker, 1988), p. 74.

Conclusion

Same words, different worlds. Borrowing the words of Kevin Vanhoozer, the attempt has been made 'not to focus on particular points of doctrinal difference, for to do this is to lose sight of the theological forest for the trees'.[1] The 'forest' is the 'fundamental structure of the "system" of Roman Catholicism'. Some Roman Catholic 'trees' (words) have been analysed in the context of the theological 'forest' (world) of Rome in order to show how their meaning diverges from the plain biblical teaching. Though similar if not the same, the words of Roman Catholicism stem from and point to a world different from the world of the biblical gospel. In order to properly deal with Roman Catholicism, attention should be given towards understanding the theological forest in order to appreciate each single tree.

What is the Roman Catholic world then? The Roman Catholic world has two axes: the nature–grace interdependence and the Christ–church interconnection. Given its optimistic bent based on an inadequate doctrine of sin, Rome fails to properly accept the distinction between Creator and creature. Since this distinction is blurred, the Roman Church receives what ultimately belongs to the triune God alone. The church is elevated to a position that makes it something more than the biblical church and different from it. Stemming out of a non-tragic view of sin, the conviction that in significant ways the church continues the incarnation of Jesus Christ has resulted in an abnormally conflated ecclesiology. From this fundamental difference, other divergences emerge in relation to authority, biblical interpretation, salvation, the perpetual sacrifice of

---

1   K. Vanhoozer in M. Levering (with a response by K. Vanhoozer), *Was the Reformation a Mistake? Why Catholic doctrine is not unbiblical* (Grand Rapids, MI: Zondervan, 2017), p. 197.

the Mass, purgatory, indulgences, veneration of the saints, penance, papal infallibility and the mediating role of Mary. The difference between evangelicals and Roman Catholics can be found with different intensities and at various levels on several points, but given the fundamental nature of the division it can be traced in all areas of faith and practice. Words may be similar, but Rome's theological world is different.

The 'formal principle' of that world is not submission to Scripture alone, but to an acceptance of the Word of God in which Scripture sits alongside the church's Tradition and ends up being under the teaching office of the Roman Church. Not having Scripture as the ultimate authority to submit to, Roman Catholicism can only be biblically confused, twisted, ambiguous and, ultimately, erroneous. Each of its uses of Scripture, however linguistically adherent to the Bible from which it borrows its words, is crossed by a principle contrary to the Word of God.

The 'material principle' of its world is not the grace of God received by faith alone which saves the sinner, but a sophisticated system that merges divine grace with the performance of the person through the reception of the sacraments of the church. Roman Catholicism speaks of 'sin', 'grace', 'salvation', 'faith'. Using these words, it employs them not according to their biblical meaning but by bending them according to its own sacramental system. The words are the same but, not being defined by Scripture, their meaning is fraught with internal deviations that make them phonetically equal to and theologically different from the Christian faith.

Some distortions of Roman Catholicism are obvious, as in the case of Marian dogmas without biblical support, or the case of the institution of the papacy which is the child of the Roman Empire, or the case of devotions that are drawn from pagan practices. Others are subtler and more sophisticated, as in the case of doctrinal 'developments' which have accrued over the centuries, or the Roman Catholic ecclesiology or view of salvation.

This means that the great bullet points of the Protestant Reformation, namely Scripture alone, Christ alone, grace alone, are all biblical remedies against the idolatrous tendency of a self-referential church, which sadly have been rejected so far. In this respect, it may be helpful to recall the document *An Evangelical Approach towards Understanding Roman Catholicism* issued by the Italian Evangelical Alliance in 1999. Here are some pertinent points which can be useful to close with:

> The doctrinal agreement between Catholics and Evangelicals, which is expressed in a common adherence to the Creeds and Councils of the first five centuries, is not an adequate basis on which to say that there is an agreement concerning the essentials of the Gospel. Moreover, developments within the Catholic Church during the following centuries give rise to the impression that this adherence may be more formal than substantial.[2]

Formally the Roman Catholic words are the same. Substantially they are not. Therefore, the call to stand for biblical truth is as urgent as ever. While every believer must continue to pray for a biblical reformation to run through individual lives and church communities, even the reformation of Rome according to the gospel is not impossible in the hands of God. Humanly speaking, it is frankly improbable and implausible, but God is sovereign and is able to do 'far more abundantly than all that we ask or think' (Eph. 3:20).

While we stand under God's providence, both ordinary and extraordinary, and trust his ways for the future of Christianity, it is important for evangelical Christians to be aware of where Roman Catholicism stands in its official teaching and outlook and what are its trajectories in the global community. This is the reason why educating pastors, churches and individuals on exegeting Roman Catholicism from a biblical perspective is vitally important. The kind of education needed is not only on individual aspects but on the whole Roman Catholic system.[3] Rome is more than its doctrines

---

2   'An evangelical approach towards understanding Roman Catholicism', *Evangelicals Now* (December 2000), pp. 12–13.
3   In this regard, useful resources can be found at <www.reformandainitiative.org> and <www.vaticanfiles.org>.

and practices taken in isolation. It is a world view – with doctrinal, political and institutional dimensions – and as such it needs to be addressed.

In so doing, dialogue with Roman Catholics must be pursued at all levels: from theological dialogue with Catholic priests and intellectuals to discussions with our Catholic neighbours or colleagues or family members. The differences that exist, no matter how deep, do not impede a friendly conversation on what really matters in our lives. Always trying to point to the Bible and trusting the work of the Holy Spirit, our task should be characterized by an openness to talk, ask questions, give answers and share lives.

Acknowledging that 'the Lord knows those who are his' (2 Tim. 2:19), the Italian Evangelical Alliance's document is again worth quoting:

> God's grace is at work in men and women who, although they may consider themselves Catholics, trust in God alone, and seek to develop a personal relationship with him, read the Scriptures and lead a Christian life. These people, however, must be encouraged to think through the issue of whether their faith is compatible with membership of the Catholic Church. They must be helped to examine critically residual Catholic elements in their thinking in the light of God's Word.[4]
> (n. 12)

All women and men are called to return to God the Father, who manifested himself in the person and work of Jesus Christ through the power of the Holy Spirit, to be saved and to relearn how to live under the authority of the Bible for the glory of God alone.

---

4 'An evangelical approach towards understanding Roman Catholicism', n. 12.

Appendix 1
Is the Reformation over?
A statement of evangelical convictions

The following is a statement released in 2016 by the Reformanda Initiative (<www.reformandainitiative.org>) on the eve of the five hundredth anniversary of the Protestant Reformation. It was translated into several languages (Italian, Spanish, Swedish, Polish, Slovakian, Portuguese, French, Romanian) and signed by hundreds of evangelical leaders around the world. It contains a strong argument for the continuing relevance of the Protestant Reformation, especially as far as the relationship with Roman Catholicism is concerned. See <www.isthereformationover.com>.

* * *

On the eve of the five hundredth anniversary of the Protestant Reformation, evangelical Christians around the world have the opportunity to reflect afresh on the legacy of the Reformation, both for the worldwide church of Jesus Christ and for the development of gospel work. After centuries of controversies and strained relationships between evangelicals and Catholics, the ecumenical friendliness of recent times has created ripe conditions for some leaders in both camps to claim that the Reformation is all but over – that the primary theological disagreements that led to the rupture in Western Christianity in the sixteenth century have been resolved.

Why some argue that the Reformation is over
Two main reasons are generally cited in support of the claim that the Reformation is over:

123

1 The challenges for Christians worldwide (e.g. secularism and Islam) are so daunting that Protestants and Catholics can no longer afford to remain divided. A unified witness (with perhaps the pope as the leading spokesman?) would greatly benefit global Christianity.

2 The historical theological divisions (e.g. salvation through faith alone, the ultimate authority of the Bible, the primacy of the bishop of Rome) are considered matters of legitimate difference in emphasis, but not sharp points of division and contrast that prevent unity.

The cumulative force of these arguments has softened the way some evangelicals understand and evaluate the Roman Catholic Church.

It is also important to note that in the last century, global evangelicalism has grown at an explosive rate while Roman Catholicism has not. The fact that millions of Catholics have become evangelicals in recent years has not gone unnoticed by Roman Catholic leaders. They are seeking to respond strategically to this loss of their faithful by adopting traditional evangelical language (e.g. 'conversion', 'gospel', 'mission' and 'mercy') and establishing ecumenical dialogues with churches they once condemned. There are now more friendly relationships and opportunities for dialogue between Catholics and Protestants where once there was persecution and animosity. But the question still remains: have the fundamental differences between Catholics and Protestants/evangelicals disappeared?

Is the Reformation over?

In all its varieties and at times conflicting tendencies, the Protestant Reformation was ultimately a call to (1) recover the authority of the Bible over the church and (2) appreciate afresh the fact that salvation comes to us through faith alone.

As was the case five centuries ago, Roman Catholicism is a religious system that is *not* based on Scripture alone. From the Catholic perspective, the Bible is only one source of authority, but it does not stand alone, nor is it the highest source. According to this view, tradition precedes the Bible, is bigger than the Bible, and is not revealed through Scripture alone but through the continuing teaching of the church and its current agenda, whatever that may be. Because Scripture does not have the final say, Catholic doctrine and practice remains open-ended, and therefore confused at its very core.

The Roman Catholic theological method is powerfully illustrated by Rome's promulgation of three dogmas (i.e. binding beliefs) with no biblical support whatsoever. They are the 1854 dogma of Mary's immaculate conception, the 1870 dogma of papal infallibility and the 1950 dogma of Mary's bodily assumption. These dogmas do not represent biblical teaching and in fact clearly contradict it. Within the Catholic system, this does not matter because it does not rely on the authority of Scripture alone. It may take two millennia to formulate a new dogma, but because Scripture does not have the final say, the Catholic Church can eventually embrace such novelties.

On the doctrine of salvation, many are under the impression that there is a growing convergence regarding justification by faith and that tensions between Catholics and evangelicals have eased considerably since the sixteenth century. At the Council of Trent (1545–63), the Roman Catholic Church reacted strongly against the Protestant Reformation by declaring 'anathema' (cursed) those who upheld justification by faith alone, as well as by affirming the teaching that salvation is a process of cooperating with infused grace rather than an act grounded in grace alone through faith alone.

Some argue that the *Joint Declaration on the Doctrine of Justification* signed by the Roman Catholic Church and the Lutheran World Federation in 1999 has bridged the divide. While the document is at times friendly towards a more biblical understanding of justification, it explicitly affirms the Council of Trent's view of justification. All of its condemnations of historic Protestant/evangelical convictions still stand; they just do not apply to those who affirm the blurred position of the *Joint Declaration*.

As was the case with Trent, in the *Joint Declaration* justification is a process enacted by a sacrament of the church (baptism); it is *not* received by faith alone. It is a journey that requires contribution from the faithful and continual participation in the sacramental system.

There is no sense of the righteousness of God being imputed by Christ to the believer and thus there can be no assurance of salvation. Moreover, the Roman Catholic Church's view is revealed by its continued use of indulgences (i.e. the remission of the temporal punishment for sin allotted by the church on special occasions). It was the theology of indulgences that triggered the Reformation, but this system has been invoked most recently by Pope Francis in the 2015–16 Year of Mercy. This shows that the Roman Catholic Church's basic view of salvation, which is dependent on the mediation of the church, the distribution of grace by means of its sacraments, the intercession of the saints, and purgatory, is still firmly in place, even after the *Joint Declaration*.

Looking ahead

What is true of the Roman Catholic Church as a doctrinal and institutional reality is not necessarily true of individual Catholics. God's grace is at work in men and women who repent and trust in God alone, who respond to God's gospel by living as Christian disciples, and who seek to know Christ and make him known.

However, because of its unchecked dogmatic claims and complex political and diplomatic structure, much more care and prudence should be exercised in dealing with the institutional Catholic Church. Current initiatives to renew aspects of Catholic life and worship (e.g. the accessibility of the Bible, liturgical renewal, the growing role of the laity, the charismatic movement) do not indicate, in themselves, that the Roman Catholic Church is committed to substantive reform in accordance with the Word of God.

In our global society, we encourage cooperation between evangelicals and Catholics in areas of common concern, such as the protection of life and the promotion of religious freedom. This cooperation extends to people of other religious orientations and ideologies as well. Where common values are at stake regarding ethical, social, cultural and political issues, efforts made towards collaboration are to be encouraged. However, when it comes to fulfilling the missionary task of proclaiming and living out the gospel of Jesus Christ to the whole world, evangelicals must be careful to maintain clear gospel standards when forming common platforms and coalitions.

The position we have articulated is a reflection of historic evangelical convictions with its passion for unity among believers in Jesus Christ according to the truth of the gospel.[1] The issues that gave birth to the Reformation five hundred years ago are still very much alive in the twenty-first century for the whole church. While we welcome all opportunities to clarify them, evangelicals affirm, with the Reformers, the foundational convictions that our final authority is the Bible and that we are saved through faith alone.

---

1 These fundamental convictions are expressed in official papers by the two global evangelical organizations: the World Evangelical Fellowship and the Lausanne Movement. After addressing such topics as Mariology, authority in the church, the papacy and infallibility, justification by faith, sacraments and the Eucharist, and the mission of the church, the World Evangelical Fellowship's summary comment was, 'Cooperation in mission between Evangelicals and Catholics is seriously impeded because of "unsurmountable" obstacles' (World Evangelical Fellowship, 'Evangelical perspective on Roman Catholicism' [1986], in Paul G. Schrotenboer [ed.], *Roman Catholicism: A contemporary evangelical perspective* [Grand Rapids, MI: Baker, 1988], p. 93). We see this view mirrored in the 1980 'Lausanne occasional paper 10 on Christian witness to nominal Christians among Roman Catholics' and a comment by the primary author of the Lausanne Covenant, John Stott: 'We are ready to co-operate with them (Roman Catholics, Orthodox or Liberal protestants) in good works of Christian compassion and social justice. It is when we are invited to evangelise with them that we find ourselves in a painful dilemma for common witness necessitates common faith, and co-operation in evangelism depends on agreement over the content of the gospel' (Lausanne Committee for World Evangelization, 'Lausanne occasional paper 10 on Christian witness to nominal Christians among Roman Catholics' [Pattaya, Thailand, 1980]; John Stott, *Make the Truth Known: Maintaining the evangelical faith today* [Leicester: UCCF Booklets, 1983], pp. 3–4).

Appendix 2
Nine key people you should know to understand Vatican II

The Second Vatican Council (1962–5) is widely regarded as the most significant event of the Roman Catholic Church in the twentieth century. In many ways it was a watershed moment that was preceded by a long period of preparation and followed by a tumultuous aftermath. Everything that Roman Catholicism is today must be read and assessed through the lenses of Vatican II. This is what this book has tried to do, namely to look at Roman Catholicism with an appreciation of its long historical trajectory but always focusing on its Vatican II and post-Vatican II outlook.

The following theologians contributed to the shaping of the theological mindset of Vatican II and/or embodied its 'spirit' so as to become seminal voices of present-day Roman Catholicism. Obviously, the list is selective, but hopefully it is also representative.[1] Its purpose is to highlight the main idea (or ideas) that each theologian has instilled in Rome's outlook, noting how the person's contribution is distinctively 'Roman' and 'Catholic' at the same time, perhaps in a different balance from that of previous ages of the church but still making Roman Catholicism what it is.

John Henry Newman (1801–90)

Newman paved the way for a dynamic understanding of tradition while maintaining the idea that Roman Catholicism is an organic

---

1 For an overview see F. Kerr, *Twentieth-Century Catholic Theologians* (Oxford: Blackwell, 2007); R. E. Gaillardetz (ed.), *The Cambridge Companion to Vatican II* (Cambridge: Cambridge University Press, 2020); D. Ford with R. Muers (eds.), *The Modern Theologians: An introduction to Christian theology since 1918*, 3rd edn (Oxford: Wiley-Blackwell, 2005); M. Seewald, *Dogma in Wandel: wie Glaubenslehren sich entwickeln* (Freiburg: Herder, 2018).

and living whole. In his *Essay on the Development of Christian Doctrine*, he often uses the category of 'system' and applies it to Roman Catholicism.[2] He argues that 'the Catholic doctrines . . . are members of one family, and suggestive, or correlative, or confirmatory, or illustrative of each other'.[3] Roman Catholicism is, as a matter of fact, 'one integral religion'[4] made up of several beliefs but marked by wholeness and indivisibility; in other words, it is the 'Catholic system'.[5] The organic relationship which unites all doctrines is stretched to the point where, if someone is confronted with it, he or she 'must accept the whole or reject the whole'.[6] In Newman's perspective as it is presented in the *Essay*, Roman Catholicism is a system not only in its merely theological dimension but also as a divinely appointed institution whose historical operations are directed by the divine Presence; in this sense, Newman speaks more specifically of the 'Roman system'.[7]

The developmental nature of the Roman Catholic system is Newman's basic apologetical argument for counteracting Protestant accusations that describe Roman Catholicism as a progressive corruption of the genuine Christian faith or as a rigid monolith. On the contrary, according to Newman, Roman Catholicism is the 'true development' of authentic Christianity and this 'development' is what energizes its life and activities.

Romano Guardini (1886–1968)

Romano Guardini is associated with the idea according to which Roman Catholicism is a *Weltanschauung* (world view), indeed the 'katholische Weltanschauung'. In the work that would become a sort of manifesto of his long teaching career as well as part of the name of his chair, Guardini outlines his understanding of 'world view'. According to Guardini, the Roman Catholic world view is not

---

2 See e.g. J. H. Newman, *An Essay on the Development of Doctrine* (London: James Toovey, 1845), pp. 135, 137, 156, 337, 369, 388, 396, 447, 449, 452.
3 Newman, *Development of Doctrine*, p. 154.
4 Newman, *Development of Doctrine*, p. 155.
5 Newman, *Development of Doctrine*, pp. 433, 446.
6 Newman, *Development of Doctrine*, p. 154.
7 Newman, *Development of Doctrine*, p. 366.

an ideology to be contrasted with others as if it were competing in an ideological struggle. It is rather an overall perspective marked by openness and universality towards the world. Since 'the catholic element is not a type beside others', it 'embraces all typical possibilities, as it embraces life itself'.[8] This aura of comprehensiveness – whose only adversary is negation – does not derive from a syncretistic attitude but from the catholic 'original essential totality'[9] in its perspective on the whole world.

In a telling sentence, Guardini links world view and institution by saying that the Catholic *Weltanschauung* fits the Roman Church because 'she is the historical bearer of Christ's plenary view of the world'.[10] Because of Christ's unique inhabitation which permeates the church, the Catholic *Weltanschauung* is 'the Church's view of the world, in faith, from the point of view of the living Christ and in the fullness of its totality transcending any type'.[11]

Yves Congar (1904–95)

Yves Congar is behind much of the U-turn that Rome has gone through on its ecumenical trajectory. From being antagonistic and even inimical to the ecumenical movement at the beginning of the twentieth century, Rome's posture changed dramatically with Vatican II, making it a full participant in that movement. Congar provided much theological thought to make the change happen. In his *Divided Christendom* (orig. Paris, 1937)[12] he sparked the idea that in non-Roman Catholic churches there are true elements of the church – elements that the Roman Church has in full measure. In *True and False Reform in the Church* (orig. Paris, 1950),[13] while setting the catholic parameters for organic change within the church

---

8 R. Guardini, *Von Wesen katholischer Weltanschauung* (1924). In the following discussion, quotations are taken from an Italian edition of Guardini's book: *La visione cattolica del mondo* (Brescia: Morcelliana, 1994), pp. 41–42; translations from the Italian into English are my own.
9 Guardini, *La visione cattolica*, p. 42.
10 Guardini, *La visione cattolica*, p. 44.
11 Guardini, *La visione cattolica*, p. 45.
12 English edn: *Divided Christendom: A Catholic study of the problem of reunion*, tr. M. A. Bousfield (London: Centenary Press, 1939).
13 English edn: *True and False Reform in the Church*, tr. P. Philibert (Collegeville, MN: Liturgical Press, 2011).

(e.g. the primacy of love and pastoral concern, communion with the church, patience, renewal through retrieval of tradition), he also reintroduced the word 'reform', albeit 'true reform' in Roman Catholic vocabulary.

Vatican II's decree on ecumenism, *Unitatis Redintegratio* (1964), contains Congar's dearest themes: the importance of 'dialogue' among Christians, the emphasis on 'spiritual ecumenism' (e.g. common prayer), the need of 'reform' in all Christian traditions, and the recognition of the elements of truth and grace in non-Catholic communities.

Karl Rahner (1904–84)

The Second Vatican Council (1962–5) significantly changed the understanding of the meaning of the dictum *extra ecclesiam nulla salus* (outside the church there is no salvation), giving rise to a 'gradualist' view of Christianity. People who follow other religions, even if far away from Christianity, are not considered away from Christ. Roman Catholicism is seen as a completion, the achievement of aspirations that already exist in non-Christian religions. Every man and woman is somewhat mysteriously associated with the 'Paschal mystery' (*GS* 22).

Roman Catholic theologian Karl Rahner's 'anonymous Christianity' is an example of this position:

> Therefore no matter what a man states in his conceptual, theoretical, and religious reflection, anyone who does not say in his heart, 'there is no God' (like the 'fool' in the psalm) but testifies to him by the radical acceptance of his being, is a believer . . . And anyone who has let himself be taken hold of by this grace can be called with every right an 'anonymous Christian.'[14]

'Anonymous Christianity' means that a person lives in the grace of God and therefore is a Christian, whether or not he or she is aware of it, and attains salvation 'outside of explicitly constituted

---

14 K. Rahner, *Theological Investigations*, vol. 6, tr. K. and B. Kruger (Baltimore, MD: Helicon, 1969), p. 395.

Christianity'.[15] Although the expression is not part of the magisterial language of Rome, its theological vision is very much behind its present-day 'catholic', all-embracing outlook.

Henri-Marie de Lubac (1896–1991)

With Vatican II, Roman Catholicism repositioned itself with regard to its appreciation of tradition, no longer looking at it as a rigid grid but rather as a living and expanding trajectory. Building on his expertise in patristics and coupling it with a passion for 'ressourcement' (i.e. retrieval of sources), de Lubac encouraged his church to expand its self-understanding from mere juridical–sociological categories to prevailing mystical ones. His influence on major Vatican II documents such as *Dei Verbum, Lumen Gentium* and *Gaudium et Spes* is evident.

Here is how de Lubac saw the nature of Roman Catholicism:

> To see in Catholicism one religion among others, one system among others . . . is to mistake its very nature . . . Catholicism is religion itself. It is the form that humanity must put on in order finally to be itself. It is the only reality which involves by its existence no opposition.[16]

Facing possible pushback to this stretched version of catholicity, de Lubac argues that 'it is neither naïveté, nor syncretism, nor liberalism; it is simply Catholicism'.[17] After Vatican II, Roman Catholicism no longer wants to emphasize its sharp and exclusive edges but rather its generous and inclusive platform.

Hans Urs von Balthasar (1905–88)

Balthasar's reflection on the 'distinctively catholic'[18] can be thought of as belonging to the same stream of reflection to which Guardini

---

15 P. Imhof and H. Biallowons (eds.), *Karl Rahner in Dialogue: Conversations and interviews, 1965–1982* (New York, NY: Crossroads, 1986), p. 207. For an evangelical assessment of Rahner, see C. M. Bucey, *Karl Rahner* (Phillipsburg, NJ: P&R, 2019).

16 H. de Lubac, *Catholicism: Christ and the common destiny of man* (orig. 1947), tr. L. C. Sheppard and E. Englund (San Francisco, CA: Ignatius Press, 1988), p. 298.

17 De Lubac, *Catholicism*, p. 302.

18 H. U. von Balthasar, *In the Fullness of Faith: On the centrality of the distinctively catholic*, tr. E. T. Oakes (San Francisco, CA: Ignatius Press, 1988).

contributed in his discussion on the Roman Catholic *Weltanschauung*. The incipit of his work *In the Fullness of Faith* ('Catholic is a quality. It means totality and universality')[19] is highly significant. Here again, what pertains to the church is seen as the 'radiation' of divine totality and universality. In other words, because 'Jesus is catholic' and 'God's love is catholic',[20] the church is also catholic in its intrinsic nature and in all its manifold expressions.

According to von Balthasar, the church 'is the pure radiation of Christ and, in order to radiate, it must also be a structure. It is both in motion "away from itself" and abiding "in itself".'[21] Therefore, it reflects and embodies the dynamics between the Roman and the Catholic aspects of Roman Catholicism. Present-day Roman Catholicism has been greatly influenced by Balthasar's recovery of the fullness of beauty, truth and goodness associated with Roman catholicity, away from neo-scholastic, narrow-minded and rigid schemes of thought.

Karol Wojtyla – John Paul II (1920–2005)

John Paul II (1978–2005) was the genial interpreter of Vatican II, conservative in doctrine and morals, and progressive in social issues and world appeal. With him, the Roman Catholic Church regained centrality in the world, relaunching the task of a 'new evangelization' and Catholic presence. Whereas the pre-Vatican II church was living through a process of gradual decay, it was revitalized by this proactive pope and encouraged to recover centre stage in the world.[22]

John Paul produced several encyclicals. On specific contents, *Fides et Ratio* (Faith and Reason, 1998) combines Aristotelian reason and Thomistic faith, a choice that leaves out many biblical strands. *Ecclesia de Eucharistia* (The Church from the Eucharist, 2003) reinforces the traditional Roman Catholic doctrine of the sacrificial nature of the Eucharist, its re-enactment of Jesus' death and the practice of adoration of the host. *Ut Unum Sint* (That They May Be

---

19 von Balthasar, *Fullness of Faith*, p. 13.
20 von Balthasar, *Fullness of Faith*, pp. 27, 31.
21 von Balthasar, *Fullness of Faith*, p. 47.
22 See T. Perry (ed.), *The Legacy of John Paul II: An evangelical assessment* (Downers Grove, IL: IVP Academic, 2007).

One, 1995) claims that the pope is willing to change the forms of his universal ministry but not the substance of his Petrine office, which supplements the headship of Christ over the church. *Redemptoris Mater* (The Mother of the Redeemer, 1987) is a Marian-centred retelling of salvation history, something that the Bible does not encourage. Moreover, John Paul's personal motto was *totus tuus* (totally yours), with 'yours' referring to Mary. A Thomistic philosopher and charismatic leader, Wojtyla in his pontificate embodied the 'aggiornamento' (i.e. updating) that was encouraged by Vatican II without losing the organic ties with tradition.

Joseph Ratzinger – Benedict XVI (1927–)

Ratzinger's theology magnificently epitomizes the catholicity of Roman Catholicism in its post-Vatican II outlook.[23] In his theology the Bible is always read in the light of the authoritative magisterium. Nicene Christology is always intertwined with 'objective' Roman Catholic ecclesiology. The Apostles' Creed is confessed, as well as the canons of Trent and Vatican I. The cross of Christ is always related to the representation of the sacrifice of the Eucharist. The Spirit is always linked to the hierarchical structure of the church. Ecumenism is always thought of in terms of other Christians being defective and the Church of Rome being the 'catholic' church. The mission of the church is always pursued while having in mind the catholic project to embrace the whole world. The ecclesiastical outlook of the church is inherently combined with its political role.

The motto of the theological journal *Communio* with which Benedict has been associated since 1972 neatly sums up his theological vision: 'a program of renewal through the return to the sources of authentic tradition'. In other words, aggiornamento is done through ressourcement (i.e. the fresh rereading of biblical and patristic sources) since the two belong together.

---

23 L. De Chirico, 'Progressive, conservative or Roman Catholic? On the theology of Joseph Ratzinger in evangelical perspective', *Perichoresis* 6.2 (2008), pp. 201–218; T. Perry (ed.), *The Theology of Benedict XVI: A Protestant appreciation* (Bellingham, WA: Lexham Press, 2019).

Jorge Mario Bergoglio – Francis (1936–)

Pope Francis is the first pope not to have taken part in Vatican II; nevertheless he embodies its vision.[24] He wants to build on John Paul II's global catholicity while shifting emphasis from Wojtyla's doctrinal rigidity to more inclusive patterns. He pays lip service to Ratzinger's rational catholicity but wants to move the agenda from Western ideological battles to 'human' issues which find appeal across the global spectrum. If Ratzinger wanted to mark the difference between the church and the world, Francis tries to make the two overlap. In shaping the new catholicity, he seems closer to the 'pastoral' tone of John XXIII, who was canonized (i.e. declared a 'saint') in 2014. So there is continuity and development. This is the gist of catholicity.

Francis has little time for 'non-negotiable' truths, and gives more attention to the variety of conscience found among different people. He is more interested in warmth than light, more in empathy than judgment. He focuses on attitude rather than identity, and on embracing rather than teaching. He underlines the relational over the doctrinal. For him proximity is more important than integrity. Belonging together has priority over believing differently. Reaching out to people comes before calling them back. Of course in all these pairings, the qualities are not pitted against each other, but their relationship is worked out within a new balance whereby the first one determines the overall orientation. Roman catholicity works this way: never abandoning the past, always enlarging the synthesis by repositioning the elements around the Roman centre. Francis calls this catholicity 'mission', and this word lies at the heart of his theological vision. The word is familiar and intriguing for Bible-believing Christians, yet one needs to understand what he means by it beyond what it appears to mean on the surface.

---

24 See my 'A window into the theological vision of Pope Francis', *Christian Research Journal* 38.6 (2015), pp. 12–19; Spanish edn: 'Una ventana a la visión teológica del Papa Francisco', in *Soli Deo gloria: aspectos y legado del pensamiento evangélico de José Grau* (Ciudad Real: Editorial Peregrino, 2016), pp. 103–113.

Appendix 3
Why evangelicals must engage with Roman Catholicism

As I speak to different audiences and at various conferences, the question comes back over and over again: why should evangelicals bother engaging with Roman Catholicism? Let me suggest four reasons.

It's a global issue

Wherever you go in the world – north and south, east and west – you will find people who call themselves Roman Catholics, and most of us interact with them in one way or another on matters of faith. You will also encounter the Roman Catholic Church through its institutions and agencies: parishes, schools, hospitals, charities, movements and so on. According to the 2020 edition of the Pontifical Yearbook, Catholics around the world amount to 1.329 billion people, comprising by far the largest religious family within Christendom and the biggest religious organization on the planet. The pope, though living in Rome, is a global figure who attracts a lot of attention from the media. The Roman Church, through its documents and initiatives, is a world-level player in major debates related to interfaith relationships, mission, the environment, ecumenism and so on. Whether you live in a majority Roman Catholic region or in an area where Catholics are few, the presence of the Roman Catholic Church is pervasive. Unless you crouch in your little corner, not wanting to engage with the world around you (wherever you are), you must deal with Roman Catholicism.

It's a theological issue

In the sixteenth century, the Protestant Reformation was a movement of God that recovered and reaffirmed the biblical gospel centred on the authority of the triune God in biblical revelation ('Scripture alone'); the sufficiency of the work of Jesus Christ ('Christ alone'); the free gift of salvation for those who believe ('faith alone'); and the call to live for God and worship him in whatever we do ('to God alone be the glory'). Roman Catholicism stood against these truths and condemned those who embraced them. After Vatican II, Rome has somewhat changed its posture; the tones are friendlier and the lines are blurred. However, Roman Catholicism is still *not* committed to Scripture alone, Christ alone or faith alone, and its devotions are not dedicated to God alone. The Roman Catholic gospel is *different* from the biblical one. None of the non-biblical dogmas, practices and structures of the Roman Catholic Church have been obliterated, although they may have been reframed or developed. The Reformation is not over, the gospel is still at stake, and all those who want to stand firm in the truth should grasp at least something of what Roman Catholicism stands for.

It's an evangelistic issue

Because of the massive number of Roman Catholics around the world, there is a high probability that all of us have Catholic neighbours, friends, family members and colleagues. In majority Roman Catholic contexts, this often means that people identify themselves as Catholics because they were born into a religious family or because the cultural milieu they live in was shaped by Roman Catholicism, but there is no basic gospel awareness. Many nominal Catholics believe and behave like most Western secular people: without any sense of God being real and true in their lives. In other words, they are not born-again, regenerated Christians. Other Catholics are religiously committed, yet they may be entangled in traditions and practices that are far from the biblical faith. This brings wide-open evangelistic opportunities. The gospel can and must be taken to them too. We must try to enter the Roman Catholic mindset and gently challenge it with the gospel. In order to do so in a spiritually intelligent way, we must come to terms with what Roman Catholicism is all about.

It's a strategic issue

Roman Catholicism brings a further challenge to evangelicals today. In the past, Rome considered other forms of Christianity (e.g. Eastern Orthodoxy and Protestantism) as heretical or schismatic; it was Rome that distanced outsiders from itself. After Vatican II (1962–5) these faith traditions are thought of as being still defective but 'imperfectly united' with Rome. Rome has become very ecumenical, wanting to come alongside other Christians so that they can be *cum Petro* ('with Peter', i.e. in a state of peace with the Catholic Church) and *sub Petro* ('under Peter', i.e. somehow embraced by the church's structures). The same is true for other religions. Prior to Vatican II these were condemned as pagan and heathen; now they are viewed as legitimate ways to God, and their followers are called 'brothers and sisters'. Rome is working hard to bring all religions together around its leader, the pope. This is no conspiracy theory; it is the universalist agenda of present-day Roman Catholicism which has been in operation since Vatican II. Evangelicals should be aware of where Rome is going. We don't want to become part of a 'catholic' project that curtails gospel mission aimed at the conversion to Jesus Christ of people who do not believe in him. The unity we aspire to is the unity of God's people under the Lord Jesus, not the generic unity of the whole of humankind under Rome.

For missiological, theological, evangelistic and strategic reasons, evangelicals must engage with Roman Catholicism in today's world.

Bibliography

Allison, G. R., *Roman Catholic Theology and Practice: An evangelical assessment* (Wheaton, IL: Crossway, 2014).

Augustine, St, *Il Cristo totale*, ed. G. Carrabetta (Rome: Citta Nuova, 2012).

Baglioni, R., *La chiesa 'continua incarnazione' del Verbo: da J. A. Möhler al Concilio Vaticano II* (Naples: Editrice Domenicana Italiana, 2013).

Balthasar, H. U. von, *In the Fullness of Faith: On the centrality of the distinctively catholic*, tr. E. T. Oakes (San Francisco, CA: Ignatius Press, 1988).

Bannister, A., *Do Muslims and Christians Worship the Same God?* (London: IVP, 2021).

Barrett, D. (ed.), *World Christian Encyclopedia* (Oxford: Oxford University Press, 1982).

Bebbington, D. W., *Evangelicalism in Modern Britain: A history from the 1730s to the 1980s* (London: Unwin Hyman, 1989).

Bucey, C. M., *Karl Rahner* (Phillipsburg, NJ: P&R, 2019).

Carson, H., *The Faith of the Vatican: A fresh look at Roman Catholicism* (Darlington: Evangelical Press, 1996).

Carter, C. A., *Interpreting Scripture with the Great Tradition: Recovering the genius of pre-modern exegesis* (Grand Rapids, MI: Baker, 2018).

Castaldo, C., *Talking with Catholics about the Gospel: A guide for evangelicals* (Grand Rapids, MI: Zondervan, 2015).

Collins, K., and J. Walls, *Roman but Not Catholic: What remains at stake 500 years after the Reformation* (Grand Rapids: MI, Baker, 2017).

Congar, Y., *Divided Christendom: A Catholic study of the problem of reunion*, tr. M. A. Bousfield (London: Centenary Press, 1939).

——, 'Dogme christologique et écclésiologie: verité et limites d'un parallèle', in A. Grillmeier and H. Bacht, *Das Konzil von Chalkedon: Geschichte und Gegenwart*, vol. 3, 2nd edn (Würzburg: Echter Verlag, 1959), pp. 239–268.

——, *Sainte Église: études et approches ecclésiologiques* (Paris: Cerf, 1963).

——, *True and False Reform in the Church*, tr. P. Philibert (Collegeville, MN: Liturgical Press, 2011).

De Chirico, L., 'The blurring of time distinctions in Roman Catholicism', *Themelios* 29.2 (2004), pp. 40–46.

——, 'Christian unity vis-à-vis Roman Catholicism: a critique of the Evangelicals and Catholics Together dialogue', *Evangelical Review of Theology* 27.4 (2003), pp. 337–352.

——, *A Christian's Pocket Guide to Mary: Mother of God?* (Fearn: Christian Focus, 2017).

——, *A Christian's Pocket Guide to the Papacy: Its origin and role in the 21st century* (Fearn: Christian Focus, 2015).

——, 'The cross and the Eucharist: the doctrine of the atonement according to the Catechism of the Catholic Church', *European Journal of Theology* 8.1 (1999), pp. 49–59.

——, *Evangelical Theological Perspectives on Post-Vatican II Roman Catholicism* (London/Frankfurt: Peter Lang, 2003).

——, 'Not by faith alone? An analysis of the Roman Catholic doctrine of justification from Trent to the Joint Declaration', in M. Barrett (ed.), *The Doctrine on Which the Church Stands or Falls: Justification in biblical, theological, historical, and pastoral perspective* (Wheaton, IL: Crossway, 2019), pp. 739–767.

——, *Papa Francisco en perspectiva evangelica* (2017) <www.reformandainitiative.org/resources/ebook-gratuito-papa-francisco-en-perspectiva-evangelica-leonardo-de-chirico>.

——, 'Progressive, conservative or Roman Catholic? On the theology of Joseph Ratzinger in evangelical perspective', *Perichoresis* 6.2 (2008), pp. 201–218.

——, 'Same word, different worlds: the Roman Catholic doctrine of regeneration', *Credo* (July 2013), pp. 64–71.

——, 'El Vaticano II, banco de pruebas de la teología evangélica', in *Soli Deo gloria: aspectos y legado del pensamiento evangélico de José Grau* (Ciudad Real: Editorial Pelegrino, 2016), pp. 115–155.

——, 'A window into the theological vision of Pope Francis', *Christian Research Journal* 38.6 (2015), pp. 12–19; Spanish edn: 'Una ventana a la visión teológica del Papa Francisco', in *Soli Deo gloria: aspectos y legado del pensamiento evangélico de José Grau* (Ciudad Real: Editorial Peregrino, 2016), pp. 103–113.

Duffy, S., *The Graced Horizon: Nature and grace in modern Catholic thought* (Collegeville, MN: Liturgical Press, 1992).

Ford, D., with R. Muers, *The Modern Theologians: An introduction to Christian theology since 1918*, 3rd edn (Oxford: Wiley-Blackwell, 2005).

Gaillardetz, R. E. (ed.), *The Cambridge Companion to Vatican II* (Cambridge: Cambridge University Press, 2020).

Galea, R., *Nothing in My Hand I Bring: Understanding the differences between Roman Catholic and Protestant beliefs* (Kingsford: Matthias Media, 2007).

Geisler, N., and R. MacKenzie, *Roman Catholics and Evangelicals: Agreements and differences* (Grand Rapids, MI: Baker, 1995).

George, T. (ed.), *Evangelicals and the Nicene Faith: Reclaiming the apostolic witness* (Grand Rapids, MI: Baker, 2011).

George, T., and T. G. Guarino (eds.), *Evangelicals and Catholics Together at Twenty: Vital statements on contested topics* (Grand Rapids, MI: Brazos Press, 2015).

Gherardini, B., *La cattolica: lineamenti d'ecclesiologia agostiniana* (Turin: Lindau, 2011).

Greshake, G., 'Was trennt? Überlegungen zur konfessionellen Grunddifferenz', *Theologie der Gegenwart* 49 (2006), pp. 162–174.

Guardini, R., *La visione cattolica del mondo* (Brescia: Morcelliana, 1994).

Guarino, T. G., *The Disputed Teaching of Vatican II: Continuity and reversal in Catholic doctrine* (Grand Rapids, MI: Eerdmans, 2018).

Hart, D. G., *Still Protesting: Why the Reformation matters* (Grand Rapids, MI: Reformation Heritage Books, 2018).

Henry, C. F. H., *God, Revelation and Authority*, 6 vols. (Waco, TX: Word, 1976).

Hodge, C., *Epistle to the Corinthians: An exposition* (London: The Banner of Truth Trust, 1959).

Imhof, P., and H. Biallowons (eds.), *Karl Rahner in Dialogue: Conversations and interviews, 1965–1982* (New York, NY: Crossroads, 1986).

Italian Evangelical Alliance, 'An evangelical approach towards understanding Roman Catholicism', *Evangelicals Now* (December 2000), pp. 12–13; also in *European Journal of Theology* 10.1 (2001), pp. 32–35. The document was issued by the Italian Evangelical Alliance and published in several languages: Italian: 'Orientamenti evangelici per pensare il cattolicesimo', *Ideaitalia* 3.5 (1999), pp. 7–8; French: 'Le Catholicisme romain: une approche évangélique', *Vivre* 8–9 (2000), pp. 10–14, and *Fac-Réflexion* 51–52 (2000/2–3), pp. 44–49; German: 'Ein evangelikaler Ansatz zum Verständnis des Römischen Katholizismus', *Bibel Info* 59.3 (2001), pp. 10–13.

Kasper, W., *Mercy: The essence of the gospel and the key to Christian life* (Mahwah, NJ: Paulist Press, 2014).

Kerr, F., *Twentieth-Century Catholic Theologians* (Oxford: Blackwell, 2007).

Lamb, J., *Essentially One: Striving for the unity God loves* (London: IVP, 2020).

Levering, M. (with a response by K. Vanhoozer), *Was the Reformation a Mistake? Why Catholic doctrine is not unbiblical* (Grand Rapids, MI: Zondervan, 2017).

Lewis, C. S., *Mere Christianity* (London: Geoffrey Bles, 1952).

Lloyd-Jones, D. M., *The Basis of Christian Unity: An exposition of John 17 and Ephesians 4* (London: Inter-Varsity Press, 1962).

——, *The Cross: God's way of salvation* (Eastbourne: Kingsway, 1986).

——, *Roman Catholicism* (London: Evangelical Press, n.d.).

Lubac, H. de, *Catholicism: Christ and the common destiny of man* (orig. 1947), tr. L. C. Sheppard and E. Englund (San Francisco, CA: Ignatius Press, 1988).

Meconi, D. V., *The One Christ: St. Augustine's theology of deification* (Lanham, MD: Catholic University of America Press, 2013).

Menke, K.-H., *Sacramentalità: essenza e ferite del cattolicesimo* (Brescia: Queriniana, 2015).

Möhler, J. A., *Symbolism or Exposition of the Doctrinal Differences between Catholics and Protestants as Evidenced by Their Symbolic Writings* (London: Gibbings & Co., 1906).

Moloney, R., 'The doctrine of the Eucharist', in M. J. Walsh (ed.), *Commentary on the Catechism of the Catholic Church* (London: Geoffrey Chapman, 1994), pp. 259–273.

Morris, L., *The Cross in the New Testament* (Grand Rapids, MI: Eerdmans, 1965; repr. 1999).

Mulder Jr, J., *What Does It Mean to Be Catholic?* (Grand Rapids, MI: Eerdmans, 2015).

Murray, I., 'Evangelicals and Catholics Together: a movement of watershed significance?', *The Banner of Truth* 393 (1996), pp. 9–21.

Newman, J. H., *An Essay on the Development of Doctrine* (London: James Toovey, 1845).

Noll, M., and C. Nystrom, *Is the Reformation Over? An evangelical assessment of Roman Catholicism* (Grand Rapids, MI: Eerdmans, 2005).

O'Collins, G., and M. Farrugia, *Catholicism: The story of Catholic Christianity* (Oxford: Oxford University Press, 2014).

O'Malley, J., *Vatican I: The council and the making of the ultramontane church* (Cambridge, MA: The Belknap Press, 2018).

——, *What Happened at Vatican II* (Cambridge, MA: Harvard University Press, 2010).

Packer, J. I., *God's Words: Studies in key biblical themes* (Grand Rapids, MI: Baker, 1988).

Perry, T. (ed.), *The Legacy of John Paul II: An evangelical assessment* (Downers Grove, IL: IVP Academic, 2007).

—— (ed.), *The Theology of Benedict XVI: A Protestant appreciation* (Bellingham, WA: Lexham Press, 2019).

Rahner, K., *Theological Investigations*, vol. 6, tr. K. and B. Kruger (Baltimore, MD: Helicon, 1969).

Rausch, T. P. (ed.), *Catholics and Evangelicals: Do they share a common future?* (New York, NY: Paulist Press, 2000).

Saucy, M., 'Evangelicals, Catholics, and Orthodox together: is the church the extension of the incarnation?' *Journal of the Evangelical Theological Society* 43.2 (2000), pp. 193–212.

Schrotenboer, P. G. (ed.), *Roman Catholicism: A contemporary evangelical perspective* (Grand Rapids, MI: Baker, 1988).

Seewald, M., *Dogma in Wandel: wie Glaubenslehren sich entwickeln* (Freiburg: Herder, 2018).

Snell, R. J., and R. George (eds.), *Mind, Heart, and Soul: Intellectuals and the path to Rome* (Charlotte, NC: TAN Books, 2018).

Sproul, R. C., *Are We Together? A Protestant analyzes Roman Catholicism* (Sanford, FL: Reformation Trust, 2012).

Steitz, C. (ed.), *Nicene Christianity: The future of a new ecumenism* (Grand Rapids, MI: Brazos Press, 2004).

Stewart, K., 'Evangelicalism and patristic Christianity: 1517 to the present', *Evangelical Quarterly* 80.4 (2008), pp. 307–321.

Stott, J., *The Cross of Christ* (Leicester: Inter-Varsity Press, 1986).

——, *Evangelical Truth: A personal plea for unity* (Leicester: Inter-Varsity Press, 1999).

——, *Make the Truth Known: Maintaining the evangelical faith today* (Leicester: UCCF Booklets, 1983).

Subilia, V., *La nuova cattolicità del cattolicesimo* (Turin: Claudiana, 1967).

——, *The Problem of Catholicism*, tr. R. Kissack (Philadelphia, PA: Westminster Press, 1964).

Vencer, J., 'Commentary on *ECT*', in H. Fuller, *People of the Mandate: The story of the World Evangelical Fellowship* (Carlisle: Paternoster; Grand Rapids, MI: Baker, 1996), pp. 191–193.

Webster, W. D., *The Church of Rome at the Bar of History* (Edinburgh: The Banner of Truth, 1995).

Weigel, G., *Evangelical Catholicism: Deep reform in the 21st-century church* (New York, NY: Basic Books, 2013).

Wells, D., *Revolution in Rome* (Downers Grove, IL: InterVarsity Press, 1972).

Roman Catholic sources (official teaching)

Apostolic exhortation: *Evangelii Gaudium* (2013) <www.vatican.va/content/francesco/en/apost_exhortations/documents/papa-francesco_esortazione-ap_20131124_evangelii-gaudium.html>

Apostolic exhortation: *Verbum Domini* (2010) <www.vatican.va/content/benedict-xvi/en/apost_exhortations/documents/hf_ben-xvi_exh_20100930_verbum-domini.html>

Bull of indiction of the extraordinary Jubilee of Mercy: *Misericordiae Vultus* (2015) <www.vatican.va/content/francesco/en/apost_letters/documents/papa-francesco_bolla_20150411_misericordiae-vultus.html>

Catechism of the Catholic Church (London: Geoffrey Chapman, 1994) <www.vatican.va/archive/ENG0015/_INDEX.HTM>.

The Documents of Vatican II, ed. W. M. Abbott (New York, NY: Herder & Herder Association Press, 1966) <www.vatican.va/archive/hist_councils/ii_vatican_council/index.htm>.

Enchiridion symbolorum definitionum et declarationum de rebus fidei et morum, ed. H. Denzinger and A. Schönmetzer (Freiburg/Basel/Rome/Vienna: Herder, 1997).

Encyclical: *All Brothers* (2020) <Fratelli tutti (3 October 2020) | Francis (vatican.va)>.

Joint Declaration on the Doctrine of Justification (1999) <1997 Joint Declaration on the Doctrine of Justification (christianunity.va)>.